Silverlands

Silverlands

Growing Up at the Actors' Orphanage

*For Rebecca
fellow writer,
friend and "publisher"
Judy Staber*

a memoir by
Judy Staber

While the incidents in this book did happen, there may be some places where some
incidents and people have been unintentionally omitted or misplaced.

Book design by Melissa Mykal Batalin
On the cover: Noël Coward with the children at Silverlands, 1953

Printed in the United States of America
The Troy Book Makers • Troy, New York
www.thetroybookmakers.com

To order additional copies of this title,
contact your favorite local bookstore or visit www.tbmbooks.com

ISBN: 978-1-935534-846

*For the children who lived at Silverlands
in the care of The Actors' Orphanage Fund,
especially, my sister Susannah
and my oldest and dearest friend, Liz*

&

*For my family
Abby, Sherrod, Dean and Ed
Daniel and Kyle
and most of all my husband, John*

CONTENTS

ACKNOWLEDGEMENTS

MANY PEOPLE HAVE helped me with my story. First and foremost are the people who lived at Silverlands when I did and who went out of their way to share their memories. Many of their memories are in this book and each one is quoted by name (first names only if they were children, but they will know who they are). Also two "old" boys from the pre-WWII days at the Orphanage, Granville Bantock and the late Dan Taylor, whose words added so much to Chapter Four. Thank you Granville and Marianne Taylor for saying I could use them.

In England, Andrew Gordon, who believed in the book and tried to get it published even as the global economy crashed, helped me immeasurably. It was he who suggested I try this way to get my story out there. My niece, Sarah Horton, and also Richard Mangan at The Mander and Mitcheson Theatre Collection; both helped me learn more about my father. Alan Brodie gave me permission to use Noël Coward's words. My sister Susannah, whose memories were often clearer than mine, filled in the gaps of our early years. Kirsten and David Slater shared their memories of the later years. And lastly, Robert Ashby, who TACT is blessed to have as their general director, has championed my efforts and given me certain pertinent information from the archives. For Robert's kindness and because without the Actors Orphanage Fund (now TACT) who knows where I would be, a portion of my royalties shall go to The Actors' Charitable Trust.

Here in America, many friends have read different drafts over the years and shared their thoughts with me: Linda Jackson, LeslieTeicholz, Valerie von Volz, Tom Gruenewald, Susan Davies, members of my two writing groups and, all those others who read it, or parts of it, in its various guises. And in fond memory of the poet Michael Gizzi who, twenty-five years ago, taught me to believe in myself as a writer and to "write what you know and feel passionate about." The people at The Troy

Book Makers, especially Eric and Melissa, who put up with my questions and put out a great product. My daughters, Abby and Sherrod, have encouraged me all along, and my husband John, has tirelessly read and reread the various versions – copyediting as he went – and supported me as I wrestled with the best way to tell my story. Thank you all.

FOREWORD

I WROTE AN earlier version of this memoir in the late 1990s. I had been thinking about writing about my childhood for years, but motherhood, and later my career, took up my time. Then my sister Susannah began to organize the very first reunion of the Actors Orphanage to be held in Chertsey, Surrey, England in the year 2000. With my husband's encouragement, I sat down and wrote everything I could remember about growing up at Silverlands. Along the way, I was put in touch with many old 'siblings' from my childhood and they have helped to jog my memory.

The first version, photo-copied and printed, was shipped off to England to await the reunion. Many of those attending read that version. Some made comments and sent me memories of their own.

Meanwhile, friends in the States had also read that early version and told me that I couldn't *just* write about growing up in The Actors' Orphanage, since I wasn't really an orphan — as indeed most of us weren't. They said I should write about my parents, especially about my mother and her family, to explain how it was that Susannah and I had had such a childhood.

I began again. I have spent the years since that first reunion researching my family, poring through old notes and letters and rewriting this memoir, retaining much of what I had already written and remembered. I have tried to explain how it was that two little girls from an ostensibly solid English family ended up as charity children for much of their childhood.

I have chosen not to use any of the children's surnames here, to avoid any unnecessary awkwardness for those who would prefer to forget those years. There maybe places where my memory was faulty and some people have been left out or misplaced; it was all such a long time ago. If you do not know who certain British celebrities are, please *Google* them, they are all there. As for the style, I have decided to use mostly British spellings and idioms, the way I was taught at school in the 1950s.

This is my story. It is not embellished. This is how it was for me; how I remember it for those twelve and a half years when I lived and grew up at Silverlands.

Judy Staber
Old Chatham, New York, USA
Autumn 2010

*The most important things in life to me are
a close-knit family and friends.
This I learned at the Actors' Orphanage.*
— Dan Taylor 1926-2006

Home is where one starts from.
— T.S. Eliot 1888-1965
The Four Quartets, East Coker V

PROLOGUE

December 1946

Imagine being just shy of four years old and left on the doorstep of a house bigger than any you had ever seen before: a giant's house! an ogre's castle!

My earliest memory of Silverlands, the Actors' Orphanage, is arriving in a black taxi from Chertsey Station in Surrey with my sister Susannah, then aged seven, and being handed over to a forbidding man called Commander Aggitter on that doorstep by our actress mother, Joan White. I can recall no tears shed, no hugs or kisses goodbye, just the feeling of being dwarfed by the huge front entryway, the high ceilings and the very large people. Perhaps there's a remembered whiff of *Je Reviens* perfume as our mother walked down the six stone steps and into the waiting taxi without a backward glance. We watched it disappear down the oh-so-long driveway. An older boy was summoned to take our small belongings upstairs to one of the rooms on the first floor.

I suppose later that day we were introduced to the matron and to Mrs. Aggitter, and eventually, probably at the next meal, to the other children. But I don't remember that. I don't remember the time of day, or what the weather was (grey, I expect); I just remember the big-ness of it all.

It was very near the end of 1946, just days before my fourth birthday, when Susannah and I went to live at Silverlands on Holloway Hill, just outside the town of Chertsey. I was to remain there for all my childhood. I flew to America at the age of sixteen and a half, out from under the Orphanage's care at last, never to return.

~~~~~~~~

December 1994

My husband John and I have crossed the Atlantic to visit my mother and to celebrate her eighty-fifth birthday with her and my sister. My mother, after sixty-five years in the theatre, had recently moved into Denville Hall, a retirement home for elderly thespians just north of London, run by The Actors' Charitable Trust.

We were met at Heathrow Airport in the early hours of a grey Tuesday morning by a former actor turned car-for-hire driver, an acquaintance of Mother's, who drove us at a rather alarming speed through the house-packed suburbs of London. He talked non-stop in his flat London accent and, after an interminable time and the passing of several recognisable landmarks more than once, I, who was not a stranger to the far western reaches of the city, came to the conclusion that he was deliberately taking us the long way round to Northwood. This was probably on Mother's instructions so that we wouldn't arrive too early and inconvenience her. We were to stop at Denville Hall for a night before taking Mother on to Spain and my sister's village of Bedar. There, two days later, her eighty-fifth birthday would be celebrated with plenty of liquid libation, with her as the centre of attention.

The car finally turned on to the circular driveway of a charming old house surrounded by spacious lawns. Our driver pulled up to the front door, got out and pushed the front door bell. We staggered after him, exhausted by our flight, the early morning ride through London's drearier suburbs and his endless nattering. The door was opened and, as we crossed the threshold, my early life flashed before me.

Mother bustled forward to greet us with a loud "Here you are, darlings," and as I kissed her cheek I noticed, over her plump shoulder, three large, framed publicity photographs lined up on an ornately inlaid credenza in the front hall.

There they were, the three doges of my childhood: Sir Noël Coward, Lord Olivier and, as he has now been dubbed, the Baron of Richmond Hill – but, as he always will be to me, just plain Richard Attenborough.

"Well, of course," I said to myself. "Naturally. I mean after all, The Actors' Charitable Trust runs this place, just as Silverlands, my childhood home, was run by the Actors' Orphanage Fund." These peers of the theatre had once all been Presidents of the Actors' Orphanage Fund, which is now called The Actors' Charitable Trust or TACT.

We murmured "hallo" and other greetings to the various retired ladies and gentlemen of the stage who would be spending the rest of their lives with my mother. We were served tea and biscuits in a drawing room decorated with theatrical posters of bygone hits and flops. We then went upstairs to inspect Mother's room and to deposit our overnight bags in the guest suite.

Mother took the elevator, and because it was too small for three, John and I said we would walk up the stairs. Over the half landing hung a large oil portrait of a handsome, brown-haired gentleman in Elizabethan costume.

'Who's that?' asked John.

'I dunno, probably Olivier,' I muttered, climbing on up.

Then I stopped in my tracks. No, it bloody well wasn't Olivier – that portrait had hung in the front hall at Silverlands for all my childhood! That man had watched us sneak downstairs on our way to raiding the larder; he had seen us gather to hang tattle-tales on the Sneak's Chair over the front stairway's highest balustrade; he had been there when someone played Father Christmas and handed out empty gift-wrapped packages to we children for publicity photos at Christmastime; he had observed the showy arrivals and departures of our theatrical relatives on visiting Sundays, and the disappointment of those children like Norma whose parents never came; and he had witnessed some of us lined up from time to time on 'Adoption Parade'. My sister and I were spared that humiliation, but my friend Terry Mac was paraded out time after time, yet never chosen. If the man in that portrait could talk, what stories he could tell!

My curiosity was piqued. We dutifully inspected Mother's new abode and deposited our luggage in the guest suite, which was equipped with at least four 'Help I've fallen and can't get up' buttons, several 'Positively No Smoking' signs, and some fine examples of wonderfully complex plumbing.

Later that day, I met with the director of the home, Mrs. Moira Miller and, after discussing Mother's needs for her well being, I asked what she knew of the portrait on the stairs. She became quite animated and told me that she had had it researched as it had interested her, too. It was, she learned, of an actor named William Terriss and had been painted in about 1890. He was wearing his costume for *Romeo and Juliet*. Terriss had often worked in actor/manager Sir Henry Irving's Company – Irving had been the first President of the Actors' Orphanage – before forming his own band of players. On 16 December 1897, as he was entering the stage door of the Adelphi Theatre on Maiden Lane to prepare for the evening's performance of *Secret Service*, he was stabbed to death by a deranged and disgruntled actor, Richard Archer Prince.

"Interesting," I said, remembering that I had grown up with a boy named Terriss, "but where did it come from?"

'Oh,' she said, 'well, you see the Actors' Charitable Trust ran an orphanage somewhere in Surrey for the destitute children of actors and actresses. When they closed the orphanage in 1959, they had some of the rather nicer furnishings put into storage. Then, when they decided in 1965 to take over managing Denville Hall, this home for the elderly members of the profession, they brought these furnishings out of storage and put them here. That portrait came from there."

"Yes, I know," I said. "I went there! I was sure I knew that portrait. I lived at the Actors' Orphanage from 1947 until 1959. In fact, I stayed on in Chertsey after the orphanage closed to finish my O-levels at school, and I watched the movers take everything out of the house."

Her mouth fell open. I could see that she, like everyone else who ever knew of it, assumed that the children at the Actors' Orphanage had all been truly *orphans*. Surely they couldn't possibly be the children of respectable, fairly well to do, educated members of the profession like my mother!

Her curiosity piqued now, Mrs. Miller asked if I would like to walk around the ground-floor rooms and see if I recognised any pieces of furniture.

"Yes, I would," I said, and so we did.

The grand piano in the drawing room was the same one on which my room-mate Janet had practised *The Moonlight Sonata* endlessly forty years before, and where some of us, who were less proficient, had hammered out *Chopsticks*. On the wall in the same room hung a large photograph of the then Princess Elizabeth in her wedding dress, with its long train arranged to fall artfully down the steps. That used to hang in the room where the big wooden wireless set was kept and where, for years every Christmas Day, we gathered to listen to the King's, and later the Queen's, speech. In another sitting room was a portrait of that same lady, now Queen of the realm, with her corgis. That photograph had had pride of place over the magnificent oak and marble front hall fireplace at Silverlands, just across from where the portrait of William Terriss once hung. Along the passage, in the residents' library, were the same glass-fronted bookcases that had stood in the long downstairs corridor outside the dining room and the assembly room at Silverlands. In one had been kept our sweet rations, doled out in meagre portions for good behaviour after church on Sundays. In the other had been books; the only titles I could recall were a complete set of Hugh Lofting's *The Adventures of Doctor Dolittle*. Those books were not used to improve our minds, but to improve our posture and to imprint our transgressions upon our souls; for following the too-frequent punishments of bare-bottom caning, we were often instructed to fill a cardboard box with a dozen or so of these books and stand holding them on our heads outside the headmaster's office until he said, "Enough."

I asked Mrs. Miller if there was a bust of Sir Gerald du Maurier anywhere around.

She said she hadn't seen one but it might be in the attic; would I like to look?

"No, that's all right," I said. "I just wondered. Janet and I had to dust Sir Gerald every Saturday morning and we got to know him rather too well." *I didn't tell her that we used to pick our noses and stuff our own snot up Sir Gerald's nasal cavities.*

As we walked around, I spotted furniture and pictures that seemed familiar, and we chatted about life, with its twists and turns. I thought about how my life might have turned out if I hadn't been at Silverlands for all those years.

My sister had only had the benefit of Silverlands for less than four years before, with our mother's encouragement, she had moved to London and trained for the theatre. After four more years, she followed Mother to America. Her childhood was a series of stops and starts, beginning with life at home with our father, whom she had adored.

Sue was to follow in our mother's footsteps, not just in the theatre, but also in that she relinquished her four children, at very young ages, into the care of others. Our mother's grandmother had done the same, abandoning my grandfather and his sisters when they were only eight, six and four, to the care of five maiden aunts. I know it was Silverlands that gave me the sense of family and roots that has enabled me to avoid following this family trait and guide my daughters to adulthood.

For my mother 'The wheel is come full circle': she would now be spending her last years amongst these furnishings of my childhood – which should have been familiar to her too, but were not.

Mrs. Miller had met my mother on a number of occasions before Mother moved in and, because my mother was who she was, a respected veteran of sixty-five years in the theatre as an actress, director and teacher, Mrs. Miller probably could not conceive of how such a charming old lady could have put her children in an orphanage. But she did, and therein is my story.

ONE

Bare Bum Beatings

WHEN MOTHER LEFT us at the front door, Commander Aggitter ushered us, not unkindly, through the foyer and summoned John, the head boy, to take us and our small things upstairs. We followed him and our luggage, Sue clutching her Teddy and I clutching her skirt, past the grand staircase in that oh-so-grand front hall, along the corridor and up narrow back stairs, curling around the always-idle lift, to the first floor, past Matron's office-cum-clean-laundry room and out onto the long, wide upstairs corridor.

Our first bedroom was at the south end of the corridor. It was a big sunny room with two tall sash windows that looked east and a bay window at the end looking over the air-raid shelters. Six white iron bedsteads, each with a thin mattress, a thinner pillow, coarse white sheets, a blanket and counterpane were lined up along the walls. The wallpaper, in every room on this floor, had huge floral bouquets marching from the wainscoting to the ceiling with its ornate crown moulding. Every child who slept in those first floor front bedrooms has that wallpaper imprinted on their memory. I know I do. I used to count those bunches of flowers every night instead of sheep; they helped me to forget the monsters and ghosts which were surely hiding under my bed, and were probably out in the hallway too.

Commander and Mrs. Aggitter were in charge from the time we arrived until 1949. They had a daughter, Vanessa, and a black and white terrier whose name, unfortunately for me, was Judy. Whenever Judy the dog got into something disgusting, which was quite often because the boys used to encourage her to furrow into the compost heap, Commander Aggitter would bark,

'Judy, you are a foul hound!' And I, who was born feeling guilty, would cringe.

But then Liz remembers Aggitter saying,

'Get outside my office, foul hound!" to each and every misbehaving child.

Elizabeth and Caroline arrived at Silverlands in March 1947, soon after Susannah and I. Liz's earliest memory is of being led into the former ballroom and seeing Sue and I standing in front of one of the high sash windows. She remembers the room being so huge and fancy that she was quite overwhelmed by its ornate columned recesses, rococo moldings, intricate parquet flooring and high ceilings. Once we were used to it, the room simply became the Assembly room.

Sue was seven and a half, Liz was five and a half – half years being very important then – and Caroline and I were just four. Liz was to leave in 1957, long before I did, and Caroline six months before her. Sue lived at Silverlands for only about four years. At eleven, she went to London to stay at 27 Rutland Gate, the hostel the Orphanage ran for a few years for those older children who had finished school. It was a halfway house for those on their way out into the world. My sister went to Rutland Gate at such an early age because our mother was convinced Sue had great promise and *must* be trained for the stage. She had friends on the Committee (the theatre is a small world unto itself) and she persuaded them to arrange for Sue to attend the acting school in London. I'm sure the Committee agreed, in part, because Sue was a bit of a handful and the Silverlands staff had often complained about her in their reports.

Susannah did get into trouble a lot. Once she and Michael were caught in the rhododendron bushes looking at each other's private parts.

"We weren't doing any more than looking," Sue protested.

However, their parents were summoned to appear before the Committee.

Our mother said, "Let me see, Susannah is nine now. I think I was ten when I did something similar." Sue and Michael were not punished... that time.

Commander Aggitter was tall and had a paunch. A Navy man, he had been hired as Headmaster right after the war in Europe ended. To me, he seemed enormous. As a very small child when summoned I would gaze up at him to see if he was smiling, but I could only see as far as the bottom of his black waistcoat, his silver watch chain dangling across his belly.

Mrs. Aggitter was not as tall. She was rather mousey and not so imposing, but when it came to disciplining we girls, she could be just as intimidating.

The Aggitters were very keen on discipline. He punished the boys, either with slipper, belt or cane, when they misbehaved. She punished the girls and always used a bamboo switch.

There was a patch of bamboo growing against the back wall of the piggery at the end of the back drive. If Mrs. Aggitter needed a new switch, she would make us go and get one. If the switch was unacceptable, we were sent to get another. Bamboo in hand, I remember trudging up the drive, into the house and up the stairs to the Aggitters' flat. Then I would hand over the weapon, drop my knickers and grab my ankles. It was an awkward position for me as I was a rather chunky child. I was always terrified I would topple over and that would make her hit me some more.

Liz told me that Mrs. Aggitter made us little smocked dresses, but I don't remember that at all, I think Liz must have dreamt that. All I remember is her making us bend over while she administered the bamboo cane to our little bare bottoms.

One time, Liz, Sue, Caroline and I with Kenny and Carl, were playing doctors and nurses outside on the grass. Kenny was delivering a battered plastic doll from under Liz's dress and the rest of us were 'in attendance as nurses and anesthetists.' A passing staff member spotted us and, calling us 'filthy brats,' marched us to Commander Aggitter's office. Kenny and Carl had to stay there, we girls were sent upstairs to Mrs. Aggitter. The girls *never* received corporal punishment from him – some propriety was observed!

We four lined up outside Mrs. Aggitter's door, in descending order of age, to receive "six of the best." This time she had a bamboo switch on hand. Sue went in first, took down her knickers and bent over. We heard the six whistling whacks. Sue came out, red-faced, trying not to cry. Next was Liz. She went in and the sound of bamboo on flesh was heard again. Then it was my turn. I was maybe five or six. I went in, peeled down my navy blue knickers, bent over, held my ankles and stared at the carpet. If you cried, she just hit you harder, so I bit my lip. Whack! Whack! Whack! On the third whack, the bamboo cane split. But did she stop? No, she went right on whacking. I had three long cuts across my little pink bottom and they began to bleed. And they stung. I snuffled and let go of one ankle so I could wipe the tears off my cheeks with my fist.

"Get...off...my...rug!" she thundered.

She swabbed my bottom with iodine and that stung even worse. Then she sent us all downstairs to complete our punishment by standing with Carl and Kenny for an hour outside Commander Aggitter's office.

But Mrs. Aggitter must have been somewhat demoralized because Caroline wasn't caned that day. In fact, Caroline says that was the only time she ever came close. She must have been a very good little girl: either good or very devious. *The scars on my bottom finally faded away when I was in my teens. The memory has not.*

Every punishment included having to stand outside Commander Aggitter's office with a box of books in your arms or worse, on your head. Madge, Valerie and Sue, caught talking after lights out, were marched downstairs in their shifts and made to stand with those heavy boxes outside the office in the dark. When they were sure Aggitter had gone back upstairs, they put the boxes down and tried to scare each other with whispered ghost stories. They could hear Aggitter returning by the 'flip-flop' of his slippers.

Liz and Triggy crept downstairs after lights-out one night to raid the larder. They had been sent to bed without supper and were hungry. We were often hungry, then. The quickest route back to their room was through the front hall and up the main staircase. They were tiptoeing from the kitchen stairs and had just reached the front hall when they heard the approaching 'flip-flop' of Aggitter's slippers. Quickly they hid in a corner in the shadows, lying on their tummies, holding their breath and praying.

Aggitter came down the main staircase from his flat on his nightly rounds. He stopped suddenly next to the cowering girls. He seemed to be listening for something. While he stood there in the dark, the edge of his slipper was on Liz's little hand. After a long moment, he continued his rounds. As soon as he was gone, they crept back up to their bedroom, never sure whether he knew they were there.

I was once made to stand outside in the courtyard, barefoot and in my nightshirt, all because I had been sitting on my bed singing "Caroline, you'll get into trouble, you sat on a rusty bubble." A much-loathed assistant matron, yanked me off the bed, washed my mouth out with soap, called me a foul-mouthed child and sent me out into the dark, cold courtyard for an hour. *To this day I have no idea why what I was singing was rude.*

Liz and Caroline's mother was an actress and their father, a theatrical agent. Like Sue and I, after their parents' separated, the sisters came to Silverlands. Liz told me her father paid the Actors' Orphanage Fund fifty-two pounds a year for both of them. I suppose if both parents were earning they were asked to contribute something.

In 1959, in an effort to ensure that I got good marks on my O levels, Mother wrote from America to Mrs. Hollands, then General Secretary, offering to pay for a tutor. Mrs. Hollands wrote that I didn't need a tutor, but if Mother was at last able to make a contribution to the Fund, they would be happy to accept it. She didn't. Many years later, from time to time she did send a small donation to the Fund, but while we were there she contributed nothing.

When Sue and I arrived at Silverlands, quite a few older boys and girls had moved in already from the temporary lodgings at Lennox Gardens in London where they had been staying while the house was made ready for those children arriving after the war. The older girls were Carol, Mina, Rozanne, Madge and Pam who remembers those much older children who had been evacuees and returned with American accents and bobby sox. Pam went to Lennox Gardens after her theatre manager father died and her opera singer mother could no longer afford to keep her. By 1947 and 1948 most new arrivals were younger children, like Susannah and me, whose parents had come through the war either widowed or disenfranchised. Like Mother, they had kept their babies in baskets under their dressing-room tables for when the air-raid sirens sounded, or had sent their older children to live with families in the countryside, away

11

from London and the bombs. They must have been relieved to be able to leave their children in a safe place, with proper supervision, away from the madness of post-war, bombed-out London. It left them free to act in repertory theatres, or wherever they could get work, without small children in tow.

In those early years, the most important person in my life was the matron, Dorothy Irvine. We little ones called her 'Matey.' She was kind to us. Matey had many old-fashioned remedies for treating our many and various ailments. For colds and coughs, we sucked Friars Balsam on a sugar lump. In the winter months, we took a cod liver oil pill every day and sometimes a teaspoon of malt extract, to ward off influenza and encourage regularity. A cut, no matter what the size, had salt poured on it. Sue fell over one day, something we all did often, and got a huge gash on her knee. She remembered,

"Matey poured half a salt cellar on it and that really stung."

An old treadle sewing machine in the laundry room was where Matey mended many a torn garment. One Saturday morning, while some of the older girls were in there darning the boys' socks – a particularly loathsome chore, – Matey ran a sewing machine needle right through her finger. There was blood everywhere. The needle broke off in her finger and she had to go to St. Peter's Hospital across the road to have it removed.

Matey left in 1950, when I was seven, and after her we had a series of matrons, each one lasting only a few months, until Miss Rennie came in late 1952.

When not in school we children ran wild much of the time, summoned by the outside bell up in the tower for meals and chores. Once inside the house, a large brass gong announced meal times and assembly. Our little lives were ruled by bell and gong.

Before every meal the Aggitters would inspect each child's hands, both sides. If our hands were dirty we had to go and wash them, sometimes again and again, until they met with approval. If we were late, or used bad language, we were made to sit at the Defaulter's Table and given plain bread and water. We never thought much of this punishment because the other kids always saved the defaulters some food, stuffing it in their pockets or under their shirts.

Mostly we were punished for minor infractions such as talking back to a staff member, talking after lights out, swearing or swinging on the clotheslines. There was some minor shoplifting at Woolworth's in Chertsey, a few runaways, and there was the much talked about time when the Boy Scouts' hut burned down, and sometimes we were punished for no discernible reason.

Mind you, the staff members were not the only ones who meted out punishments. The older kids had their own methods. When I was six, John left and Ken succeeded him as head boy. We younger ones were as much in awe of Ken as we were of Aggitter. Some days, he'd put a chair on top of a table in the Rec' room, sit on it and make us file past and kiss his rather smelly feet.

The initiation rite for new kids was to shut them in The Den of Death, to prepare them for worse to come if they did not toe the line. The Den of Death was a room, well more of a dungeon really, underneath the inside courtyard. It was murky and smelly and festooned with spider webs, as well as other nasty things you couldn't see because it was so very dark. There was no light except for what little filtered through the grating from the courtyard above. Each victim was shoved, unceremoniously, through an old creaky doorway, down slippery stone steps, into that dark, cold, clammy room and shut in. After what felt like forever the torturers, Ken and his gang, would begin by dropping gobs of spit, worms and worse through the grating and someone would wail,

"Remember we'll always be watching yooooou. We are the ghosts of the children who didn't do as they were told. Remember us."

It was enough to scare the living daylights out of you. Fifteen minutes in that dark, dank, dungeon-like room under the courtyard, with nasty things dropped on you and terrifying sounds echoing from God-knew-where, was enough to make anyone toe the line. *And* if you happened to forget the terror of that first time and didn't do what Ken and his gang wanted, they'd put you down there again – for longer.

While the Den of Death was used to establish ground rules: to terrify new kids and let them know who was really in charge, it wasn't the worst that could happen. Woe to you if you were a tattletale, for then an example was made of you in front of everyone. The worst possible offense at Silverlands was sneaking to a staff member.

Whoever dreamed up the Sneak's Chair had an inventive and devious mind. It was never mentioned in the stories of life before the War, so I suspect it was Ken and company. I saw it used only once, when the Savage-Bailey's were in charge, right after the Aggitters left.

It was a Saturday, after chores were done and lunch was eaten. We had free time then and so did the staff. Word went out that we were all to go to the front hall. We gathered quietly in front of the fireplace not knowing what was going on. Ken stood on the lower landing looking down on us and said,

"Someone has been sneaking and other kids are getting punished because of it."

Silence.

"I know," he added grimly, "who it is."

We all looked around wondering who was guilty.

Ken suddenly signaled to four of the bigger boys. They grabbed a younger boy, a boy about seven, my age. He was a skinny, sharp-faced kid.

Before he could yell, they gagged him with a piece of rag. Then, they carried him up to the very top landing of the front hall stairs, at least twenty feet up. The kid was squirming, pale and terrified. Snot ran down his chin. They tied him to an ordinary straight-backed chair with just their belts! Those striped elastic belts with a snake clasp that were used to hold up boys' trousers. They put two around his chest and two across his lap. Then they looped some old clothesline through the back of the chair, hoisted it up in the air over the balustrade and with two boys on each rope end, they lowered him over the edge. Down below we watched dumbstruck. The boy dangled for what seemed like ages. A dark stain appeared on the front of his grey shorts.

Ken muttered, "All right," and they pulled him back up.

Then Ken turned to us and said,

"Let that be a lesson, you lot. Sneak and *you'll* get the Sneak's Chair."

I took that to heart. I learned very early on to be silent and stoic.

Ken turned fifteen the following year and left for the new London hostel at Rutland Gate. The Sneak's Chair went with him. We never saw it used again.

The boys were not the only ones to practice initiation rites and other cruelties. The girls had their own versions. In my sister's dormitory, whenever a new girl arrived, on her first night they rolled her up in her mattress and peed on her.

Caroline and I had to show our subservience to my sister's group by letting them use the lavatory first or by lowering our eyes when they passed by. For some infractions we were forced to drink glasses of pee – I don't know whose. If you were caught whispering or if they wanted information, they would take you to the outside girls' toilets off the outer courtyard and there two of them would hold you upside down over the bowl by your ankles and slowly lower you down over the whirlpool of a flushing toilet. Confessions came easily then. Sometimes they would barricade you inside one of the stalls and wouldn't let you out, or if you had to go really badly, they would prevent you going until your bladder was ready to burst.

I can actually recall quite a lot of this kind of psychological torture. My sister was particularly good at it and even used it in order to get me to do things for her, or to take the blame for something she had done when we were visiting our Grandparents. If we were playing hairdresser and she cut my hair way too short or if she broke a cup, she would say to me, " If you tell Granny I did it, I'll tell her you did it – and Granny will believe me because I am the oldest!" I believed her every time and often took the blame for things I hadn't done. It was easier that way.

The oldest girls Carol, Pam, Mina, Rozanne, Madge, Wendy and Valerie were put in charge of us little ones and I remember them all as kind. Most of them had left before I was seven. On weekends, they took us for walks or watched us while we played. I was five and riding my 'hobby horse' stick down Chestnut Avenue when I fell and a large stone became embedded in my right knee. Mina took me, howling, to the girls' toilets, popped the stone out of my leg and plopped it, all bloody, into the toilet. She then tied her handkerchief around my leg and dried my tears on her skirt. I still have the hole in my knee, just above my field hockey scars.

Pam had an odd habit of banging her left wrist against her hipbone. With my small hand clutched in hers we'd walk down the driveway saying nursery rhymes and picking flowers; suddenly she'd stop and Bang! Bang! Bang! Her wrist would be banged hard against her hip.

> *In the year 2000, we had our first, and largest, Orphanage Reunion in Chertsey. My sister Susannah had organized it with great perseverance, and somehow managed to find former orphans all over the world. Liz and I, with my husband, had come over from America. On the first day, we gathered in the bar at the Bridge Hotel in Chertsey waiting to see who would arrive next. Pam, with her husband Keith, arrived from their home in Lancashire. She took one look at Liz and me and said,*
> *'I used to bath you.' This was fifty years later!*

Every Sunday morning we Anglicans walked, two-by-two, along Lyne Lane to Trinity Church. The few Roman Catholics went to Father somebody-or-other in Chertsey. We sat on the right side of the church, crammed in six to a pew. Some of the older children were in the choir, as I would be later. In front of us, in the first two rows were the patients from Botleys' Mental Hospital. The regular parishioners sat on the other side. Forty-plus orphans and a dozen mental patients across the aisle were probably not conducive to peaceful prayer.

The pews were hard, wooden and perfect for letting loose a good triple-fart during a solemn moment in the service. It was important not to look guilty. It's hard to prove where a fart comes from when six little bodies are sitting buttock to buttock.

The parish priest in those days was Vicar Hodge, a most unappetizing man. He had bad breath; a monotonous voice and he preached long, for-gettable sermons. Once, when pounding the pulpit about the importance of our immortal souls, he took off his shoe and passed it around. *I now think he simply liked the sound of the homonym for his homily, but it made no sense and besides, his shoe smelled awful.*

One Sunday, during an interminable sermon, there was one heck of a racket coming from the back of the church. Everyone looked around. Peter and Brian began to giggle. Finally, they were laughing so loudly that Vicar Hodge stopped the service and strode down the aisle, cassock flapping, to investigate the noise. Out on the porch an old biscuit tin was jumping around like something possessed. Vicar Hodge pried it open and one very angry red squirrel leapt out. Brian and Peter were grounded for days.

Where there were animals, usually there was Brian. He saved baby birds fallen from their nests, wounded frogs, three-legged mice, even snakes. When Mrs. Aggitter found baby rabbits in Brian's bedroom, in his clothes drawer, she said,

'They will have to be destroyed, Brian. You cannot kept vermin in the house.'

Brian lost his temper and yelled,

'You are a dirty rat.'

Commander Aggitter overheard.

'He grabbed me by the neck,' Brian said, 'and marched me into the office where I had the biggest thrashing of my life. Then he gave me the longest punishment that anyone ever had. He told me I had to be in bed by 6 o'clock every day for one whole year.'

Luckily for Brian the Aggitters left Silverlands for good, just three weeks later with Brian's punishment unfulfilled. *I never knew why the Aggitters left. I remember them very dimly now.*

TWO

Before We Were a Gleam
in Our Father's Eye

OUR MOTHER, ON the other hand, had what seemed to me to have been a happy, normal childhood. Her father was chief engineer for the Eastern Telegraph Company's Mediterranean cable stations and consequently the family moved with each new posting. Mother was born in Alexandria, Egypt in 1909 and her sister, Audrey in Estoril, Portugal three years later. They grew up in Portugal, the Azores and finally Gibraltar, living in Company housing and waited on by local servants. The sisters spoke fluent Portuguese and played with the children of Company employees and, when permitted, *las filhas* from the native families.

Theirs was a sunny, uncomplicated life filled with security, beautiful scenery, voyages home to England and a glorious climate, marred only by the periodic arrival of yet another new English governess hired to teach them how to behave and to speak the King's English. Their parents, in that post Edwardian and still very colonial age, hosted and attended cocktail parties – where Grandfather earned his nickname 'Pinky White' from his love of pink gin – and went on picnic outings. My grandmother was much in demand for lawn tennis. The children were brought up by the servants and governesses, seeing their parents mostly at night for a kiss and a bedtime story, those being the days of 'children should be seen and not heard.'

Their lives were relatively untouched by World War I, 'the War to End All Wars', raging through-out Europe, even though Grandfather's role was becoming increasingly important. Laying the miles and miles of cables from England to allied European countries and across the Atlantic Ocean to the Americas had become a vital and timesaving method of communication among the Allies.

Mother's parents, Kathleen and Henry White, had each come from very different backgrounds. My grandmother was the seventh child of a well-to-do Salisbury family. Her father, William Beach, was a prominent cutler, as were both her grandfathers. She grew up surrounded by servants and older siblings with a battle-ax of a mother and a life of relative luxury. In all her married life abroad she never needed to do housework or cook. My grandfather, on the other hand, was the only son of a hard-drinking Somerset solicitor who, at thirty-five, had married a seventeen year old half-Romany gypsy girl, Emma Lee Byron Harril. They had three children, Grandfather and two younger sisters. When the children were eight, six and four years old, Emma Lee abandoned the family and disappeared. Grandfather grew up under the collective thumbs of his five maiden aunts and his alcoholic father. At sixteen he escaped to sea, first as a cabin boy, and worked his way up through the ranks of the Eastern Telegraph Company.

Was Emma Lee's abandonment of her children the first in our family tree? Did it skip a generation or was it because my grandparents' lives were so easy that neither felt the need to divorce and put their children aside at an early age? Certainly this family trait reared its head again with Mother and later with my sister. Can such behaviour be inherited?

When Mother was twelve, concerned that their daughters were becoming uneducated little heathens, my grandparents enrolled her, at her request, at a boarding school in England. (St. Helen's Northwood was less than half a mile from Denville Hall where she was to spend her last days). Mother loved St. Helen's and thrived there, unlike her sister Audrey who lasted one term and returned happily to Gibraltar for the remainder of her education.

I have no idea how much her own childhood affected our mother's decision to send us away. Perhaps Mother felt that, as she had, so would we thrive at 'boarding school', despite our very tender years and she was able to set her mind at rest with that thought.

At St. Helen's, Mother was an eager participant in all things to do with drama, winning the Poetry prize and appearing in every school play. When school was over at eighteen, she wanted nothing more than to go to the Royal Academy of Dramatic Art in London and become an actress.

Her parents, their solid yeoman heritage showing, strongly disapproved. "Nice girls did not go on the stage!" Her mother was adamantly opposed, but Mother begged, wheedled and cajoled her father until he agreed that if she could pass the stiff entrance exams, which he privately doubted, he would pay the tuition. She passed. For three years she studied voice, acting, movement, stage make-up and everything she would need to become an actress. Once on her own she would need talent, perseverance and luck.

In a passage from her memoir *Alive to Tell the Tale* Mother related that upon finishing her studies at RADA, she showed up, without an appointment, at the London flat of producer Anmer Hall. She told him, rather boldly,

"I want to join your Cambridge Festival Theatre. I can act. You can come and see me doing two different characters this week."

The Festival Theatre was breaking new ground in Cambridge with a company of up and coming actors that included Robert Donat and Flora Robson. After her performances, she went again to see him, again unannounced, demanding to know of his secretary,

"Did Mr. Hall see me act and what did he think?"

At that moment, a very tall man with startling eyebrows, wearing a rumpled grey suit, red tie and sandals without socks came out of Hall's office and, introducing himself as Tyrone Guthrie the Company's director, said,

"Mr. Hall did see you act, dear, and thought you quite good. However, we are fully cast. We can offer you an apprenticeship...that means that you don't pay us and we don't pay you."

She cheekily replied, "Isn't the labourer worthy of his hire?"

"Well dear," said Guthrie, "take it or leave it. It's good experience. A lot of hard work but, I promise you, you'll learn a lot."

She took it, joining her RADA classmate Robert Eddison as an apprentice. Robert would later play Hamlet at the Old Vic, as well as many other Shakespearean and classical roles and became a highly acclaimed actor, yet in spite of his sterling resume, he is probably most widely remembered as the ancient Grail Knight in *Indiana Jones and the Last Crusade*. Robert was to remain Mother's lifelong friend. Tyrone Guthrie, another lifelong friend, would also become her mentor. He and his wife Judith were my godparents.

For her year as an unpaid apprentice, Grandfather was once more prevailed upon to foot the bill. He paid for her lodging, her clothes and her meals. Our mother never once had to do secretarial work, wait on tables or do any other kind of temporary work that most young actors did and still do. *I know I did and during my years as an actress in New York City I had two, sometimes, three jobs to keep that proverbial wolf from my door.*

So in 1930, she put in her time as an apprentice with the Cambridge Festival Theatre and the following year she was put on salary. In 1932, the company moved into London to the Westminster Theatre. For the remainder of the decade she was rarely out of work. After one season at the Westminster, the Cambridge Festival Theatre disbanded and Mother, now out on her own, was in thirteen West End productions and three films between 1933 and 1939. Some plays were short-lived and not well received by the critics; others ran for months to rave reviews.

She played the virgin of the title in *The Synthetic Virgin* and a simple country girl in *Vacant Possession*. After a brief run in *A Present from Margate* and a much longer run in *The Golden Toy* (a spectacular production complete with elephants, dancing girls and Music Hall comics at the Coliseum), she landed the title role in *Charlotte's Progress*. The notices both for the play and for her performance were not good, although on 12 July 1934 *The Times* allowed, '...though she does not discover the play's significance for us, she speaks it with elegance.' All that RADA voice training was paying off! At the "Q" Theatre, a press release noted, 'In *The Restless Room* Miss Joan White plays the part of a girl who is frozen in a glacier crevasse for 25 years and is then restored to life.'!

Sadly, I have had to glean much of this from newspaper files and her scrapbooks, for Mother never did take the time to tell us about her successes (or failures).

In 1934, she was married for the first time to a young playwright named John Vesey Beanes, but the marriage lasted less than a year. While appearing in *The Barretts of Wimpole Street*, the producer C. B. Cochran's office telephoned to ask if she could play a sixteen year-old. Of course, she promptly said, "Yes." Washing off her makeup and putting her hair in a snood, she rushed to audition for the part of Connie Windlestraw in James Bridie's *The Black Eye*. The casting was propitious in many ways: James Bridie was to become a dear friend and supporter, and the role of Connie established her ability to play teenage girls, which she did well into her thirties.

George Bernard Shaw saw her in *The Black Eye* and leaning over to his companion, the German actress Elisabeth Bergner, said, "There's your Phebe."

She was cast as Phebe the shepherdess in *As You Like It*, which starred Bergner and the young Laurence Olivier. As one of the very first Shakespeare films, it was very well received. Bergner's husband, director Paul Czinner, had assembled an extraordinary cast, which included Henry Ainley, Felix Aylmer, Leon Quartermaine, Aubrey Mather and a very young Peter Bull. On 4 September 1936, *The Times* of London wrote:

> Sylvius and Phebe, in the hands of Mr. Richard
> Ainley and Miss Joan White, were extremely engaging
> and the whole cast is to be commended for a serious
> and often sensitive treatment of the poetry.

Mother wrote that during the filming at Elstree Studios the real sheep ate the faux foliage causing them to have loud and pungent gastric distress. Consequently all Mother's scenes had to be re-filmed resulting, as she said, in lots of lovely overtime pay.

After the success of *As You Like It*, Mother was much in demand. In *Children to Bless You* with Nigel Patrick as her brother, she played Tonie '...the nasty child in which Joan White successfully specializes,' so wrote the delightfully named critic, M. Willson Disher in *The Sunday Times*, 8 March 1936. The play opened at The Ambassadors in early March 1936 and, with excellent box office and reviews, moved to The Duke of York's later that month. The managing director of the Duke of York's was a certain A.P. Moore, who was to be my father. Children to Bless You *was such an ironic title for the play in which our parents first met, considering what was to come.*

After *Children to Bless You* came *Housemaster* by Ian Hay, both he and James Bridie were to be my sister's godfathers. *Housemaster* ran for over a year at the Apollo Theatre and cemented Mother's reputation as a 'child' actress. While she had played many young girls before, Button Faringdon the twelve year-old tomboy niece of the housemaster in the play's title, is the role that she was and still is, most fondly remembered.

> *Shortly after Mother died in 1999 and her obituary appeared in my local paper, an elderly lady stopped me on the street in Stockbridge, Massachusetts.*
> *She said, "My dear, I had no idea that the Joan White who ran The Berkshire Playhouse here, was the same one who said 'Do you mean funny peculiar or funny ha-ha?' in* Housemaster. *I saw that when I was a girl in London and I have never forgotten her in that role."*

Mother was twenty-seven when she played Button and she continued to play young teenagers until she was 34, after I was born. It was during *Housemaster* that she was formally introduced to A. P. Moore, our father to be.

In an effort to introduce foreign and little known English playwrights to interested theatregoers Father, along with a number of prominent theatre people, had formed the London International Theatre Club (LITC). The plays they selected might not have been considered commercially viable, but Father and the LITC thought them to be 'worthy of a showing.'

For two years, on Sundays when theatres were dark, *avant-garde* plays were presented, first at The Duke of York's and later at The Globe. The first to be presented was James Bridie's *Susannah and the Elders:* Bridie having written the part of Susannah for our mother. My sister was to be named after Mother's role.

> *I have always been grateful that when I was born, Mother was playing Judy Graves in* Junior Miss. *If she had been in* Housemaster *at that time, I might have had to go through life as Button!*

My sister and others have told me that my father was a handsome and charming man. Sue knew and adored him until he left when she was six; her adoration was rekindled when he reentered her life after her twenty-first birthday. She told me that I looked like him: that I have his nose, his hairline, his square jaw and his small hands and feet. She said he wasn't very tall, was very well spoken, well read and spoke five languages fluently. He was also very smooth and not above telling a lie or two to get ahead – in short, he had a touch of the 'wide boy.'

Paraphrasing *Who's Who in the Theatre*, 1939 edition, it states that A. P. Moore was born in Sligo, Ireland, went to private school and worked in the theatre in New York for Charles B. Dillingham. In actual fact, he was born and raised on the mean streets of Brixton, in South London, where his father was a cobbler and his mother took in laundry. He went to Brixton schools and, as soon as he had earned the money, he took a freighter to Chile and worked for five years as secretary at a nitrate company in Antofagasta. While there, I surmise that he remade that young man from Brixton into a well-spoken, well-read and accomplished Englishman. (I discovered this information about his journeys on manifests of Grace Line ships to and from South America in 1926 and 1931).

Back in England in 1931, possibly for his father's funeral, he applied for a job at The Duke of York's Theatre, and was introduced to Violet Melnotte, its elderly owner and manager. She took a liking to him and, in a very short time he went from her assistant to Managing Director of her theatre.

According to the newspapers of the time, 'Madame' Melnotte asked Father to marry her. This caused an enormous scandal: she was fifty years his senior! Acutely aware of the damage negative publicity could do, she backed down and proposed to adopt him instead. But Violet died in 1935 before this could happen. In her will, Father was named as sole licensee of her theatre, a position he held until the outbreak of the Second World War in 1939 when he, and most other able-bodied men, enlisted and life changed forever.

In *Alive to Tell the Tale*, after having mentioned Father only briefly in connection with the London International Theatre Club, Mother wrote,

> Meanwhile, A.P. Moore and myself had decided to marry and the venue for our reception was the stage of the Duke of York's.

That is all *our mother wrote about our father in the story of her life. It is such a matter of fact sentence. I'd like to think that there was some romance, some mutual affection and a few happy days before it all went sour.*

THREE

When We Were Very Young

WHEN GERMANY INVADED Poland on 1 September 1939, Father and Mother were living at 5 Raphael Street in Knightsbridge with Susannah not quite two months old. Until her pregnancy was no longer possible to disguise, Mother had been playing yet another school-girl, Judy Bingley, in *Little Ladyship* with Lilli Palmer.

As soon as war was declared, able-bodied men rushed to enlist in the armed services to fight for King and Country. Father, who turned thirty-two that October, signed up and on 4 November 1939, unfit to fight because of poor eyesight, was appointed by the War Office as Public Relations Officer for the Western Command. By June of 1940, with the Germans targeting England, Father was given the rank of Second Lieutenant in the Gloucester Regiment and immediately promoted to the rank of Acting Captain. His job was to meet with, and release information to, members of the press corps; information fed to him by his commanding officers. For this purpose he was allowed an imprest account and thus could spend seven shillings and sixpence per head per meal.

By the autumn of 1940 the Blitz had begun and London and the Home Counties were taking a beating from the German bombers. The stage-house of Father's theatre, The Duke of York's, was hit, as were several other London theatres. With the war begun in earnest, Mother and Father gave up their tiny Raphael Street flat and moved with Susannah to the relative safety of South Moreton in Berkshire where Mother's parents, recently retired from the Eastern Telegraph Company, were living. Father was posted to Chester in the north of England. Mother and Sue stayed on with her parents and Mother helped with War Canteen work, putting on plays with village children and the evacuees from London. She wrote,

> The village children were no trouble at all but
> lacking in talent. Whereas, the Londoners were
> like belligerent sparrows, sharp and talented.

With the bombs falling closer and closer, Mother and Sue moved further north to Snitterfield, a little village just above Stratford-on-Avon in Warwickshire. There they spent six months lodging with a Farmer Cox, growing vegetables in a victory garden and collecting eggs from the chickens, all given names by Sue, now a toddler. On the moonlit night of November 14, 1940, having put Sue to bed, Mother was sitting and chatting with Farmer Cox on the porch. Looking to the northeast, they saw a tremendous fire on the horizon. She wrote later,

> In spite of the distance we clearly saw the flames and smoke
> rising. We learned later that it was the city of Coventry:
> over 500 German bombers had massed for the biggest raid
> of the war to date – their target Coventry – a city at the
> industrial heart of Britain's war production engine.

Hundreds of people were killed and almost the whole city was decimated including its magnificent Gothic cathedral.

As the weather turned colder up north, Mother and Sue moved down to Maidenhead and by mid-1941 were back in London now that the Blitz was over. Father's war work kept him out of town, but he was often able to be in London. In 1941, together they found and purchased the lease on 36 Paultons Square in the Royal Borough of Kensington and Chelsea.

Paultons Square had, and still has, one of London's charming little private gardens. Just off the King's Road, the garden had flowering trees and shrubs, beds of seasonal flowers and shaded benches by small lawns; everything lovingly tended by some of the residents. Each house on the square owned a key to this gated garden, keeping out undesirables. Every day, starched nannies with their high, shiny, black perambulators, their toddler charges firmly in hand or harness, would enter the leafy green enclosure, sit on the benches and gossip while the children played – nicely.

By September 1941 Mr. and Mrs. A. P. Moore had moved in. Number 36 was a charming Regency row house near the southeast corner of the square. Guests entering from the street went up three scrubbed-till-they-shone steps to the front door with its shiny brass lion's-head knocker, passed through the front hall and into the dining room, the front parlor or the cozy rear sitting room. The main bedrooms were one flight up and on the very top floor were Susannah's nursery and a room for Nanny.

Delivery boys and dustmen reached the kitchen by going down the stone steps behind the black wrought-iron railing. From the kitchen with its big wood-fired stove and dominant solid kitchen table, a door led onto a rear, rectangular, walled garden. In the middle stood a large laburnum tree under which Father and Sue one day solemnly buried Sue's goldfish. Purple wisteria and ivy climbed the walls. A large tabby cat adopted the new family. Susannah named him Tiger. Much to Nanny Ball's disapproval, Tiger would sit on my pram and watch over me as I slept in that walled garden under the laburnum tree.

They had hired Nanny Ball before I was born. I am sure that living at such a posh address, with daily help in the kitchen, having a Nanny was a MUST. Sue wrote to me,

> I think she (Nanny Ball) came to Paultons Square along with the house and the up-style living. I can remember Father having a chauffeur driven car and also being exceedingly handsome in his uniform. Peaked Captain's flat hat no less!

She continued,

> I remember you sliding down the stairs on your belly and consequently getting Impetigo, a nasty scabby rash and Father painting pictures of battleships on your belly with Gentian Violet. I remember Nanny taking us to the Paultons Square garden, or along the Kings Road, in that huge Silver Cross pram, with you at one end and me at t'other, and her saying that you had got Impetigo from gutter-snipes who leaned into the pram to see you. But I only got to ride when my little legs were too tired to walk.

What Sue remembers most about Nanny is how strict she was. We were both rigorously potty-trained. Being a sturdy infant, as soon as I could sit up I was made to sit on my potty immediately after breakfast and I was not allowed to get off it until I had 'done something.' It is sixty-some years later and my insides are still bound up by that infant regimentation of Nanny Ball.

Nanny Ball lived with us only until the War was over and the house was put on the market; yet she left her mark on our little minds. Sue still remembers going one day to visit Nanny Ball's home. Her father kept greyhounds locked in a big wire cage in the garden, but where it was and exactly when, she couldn't recall,

'Fragmented memory, sorry!' she said.

Memories of early childhood do come in fragments: a smell, a sound or a particular kind of day can kindle a memory, but pure memory becomes muddied with the introduction of old photographs or other people's reminiscences and suggestions. My life from birth to four is shrouded in mist, but certain things ring out clear and true when triggered.

My parents befriended Rudy, an American soldier, when we lived in Chelsea.

I remember his rough army uniform and him bringing Wrigley's chewing gum and Hershey chocolate bars for Sue and I as we sat in our safe house under the kitchen table. We were probably in the kitchen because of the nightly blackouts. I still remember the whine of the buzz bombs: in early 1945, one destroyed a row of houses behind Old Church Street, close to our house.

I have very few real memories of family life: my sister Susannah screaming after being burned by Nanny with an iron to teach her that irons were hot; the smell of my mother's perfume and the softness of her fur coat as she brushed my cheek in a good night kiss on her way to the theatre; my father, in a dark blue apron with white stripes, cutting up something in the kitchen – but perhaps that was just a fantasy, for I have been told by Sue that he liked to cook. *When you have no idea what kind of man your father was, your imagination takes over. Not ever knowing a parent leaves a rather large gap in one's make up.*

All that I have are two small black and white photographs of him. One is of an idyllic family scene in the English countryside: my sister, Father and I are in a grassy meadow, Susannah, aged about four, holds a bunch of wild flowers in her fist, Father, crouched beside her, has me, a most substantial baby on his knee. It must have been taken in the summer of 1943 for I was born that January. The other photo shows him at his desk in 1960, just two years before he was to die at fifty-five. Wearing dark-framed glasses, his hair dark and wavy, he sits behind piles of papers looking off to his right, a smile on his face, as if welcoming a visitor.

He left our family when I was two and a half. The war in Europe was finally over. No one knew, or at least ever said to us, where or why he had gone. One story, we heard later, was he had embezzled £9 to buy Sue a teddy bear; but that wasn't true. In 1960, he sent Susannah in Canada a telegram on her twenty-first birthday. She was about to give birth to her first son, Jamie. Father telegraphed that now she was twenty-one he could legally see her.

We were to learn much later, after Mother died, that she had had a restraining order put on him when he left the family. He had kept up with news of us through his brother Arthur. We never knew why Mother did this, and she would never talk about it. In our ignorance, while we were growing up, we assumed all kinds of terrible things about him. We were wrong. None of them were true.

> *I was to learn, much later on, these truths about my father: that he had been a successful theatre publicist and manager; that he had produced avant-garde plays and introduced many innovative works to London audiences. Under his aegis, in addition to* Susannah and the Elders *which starred my mother, the London International Theatre Club introduced the French playwright Jean Anouilh to England with his play* Le Voyageur sans Baggage *and, later,* Gentleman's Agreement, *an English adaptation of a Hungarian play about anti-Semitism — given what was happening in Germany, a production both controversial and timely.*
>
> *I don't know if it is in my genes, for I never knew him, but I too had a career in arts management and public relations and have helped to*

introduce new theatre works to audiences here in America. How I wish I could have talked to him about it all!

Sometime in 1942, after two and a half years of highly commended service, Father was cashiered. The charge was ostensibly for "fraudulent misapplication of imprest funds." *Having read the court transcript myself, and talked to his sister-in-law Gina, after Mother died, I am convinced he was punished for a very different reason.*

I was born six months after this unhappy time. A very large baby, ten and a half pounds, I arrived a month late. This caused the delay of *Junior Miss* rehearsals and producer Firth Shepard telephoning Mother frequently to ask, 'How's that baby coming?'

Mother had been signed to play yet another teenager in a role that would require her to spend much of the play sitting on the floor in a yoga position. She often reminded me later that she suffered considerable post-partum distress on account of my birth, but perhaps some was on account of father's troubles and the ensuing bad press.

For quite some time during the war, in spite of motherhood, pregnancy and Father's troubles, Mother had been looking to get back on 'the boards'. When she was offered the role of Judy Graves in this light American comedy in 1942, she signed on for the full run of *Junior Miss*. Her contract included a tour of the country to follow the West End engagement. The play went into rehearsal as soon after my birth (3 January 1943) as she could manage, and opened on the 23rd of March. With the constant threat of bombs falling, I was to spend much of my infancy in a laundry basket, either under our solid kitchen table or under Mother's make-up table in her dressing room at the Saville Theatre.

After I was weaned – Mother once again having to strap her bosom down – Susannah and I were evacuated to Norfolk to the foster care of Ada Pash, a large and dour country woman, who fed me rather too well on a diet of Cow & Gate powdered milk and mashed potatoes. We stayed in Norfolk for only a short time returning to London even though the buzz bombs were still falling.

The buzz bombs, or doodlebugs, made a distinct whining sound as they flew overhead. Londoners, by now inured to bombing, learned to go about their business, walking along the streets as the huge, cross-shaped, bombs flew overhead, but when the engines cut out, everybody took immediate cover in the nearest air-raid shelter or the Underground, because there was never any way of knowing where the bomb would land.

Junior Miss had been a success on Broadway and was a great favourite with the homesick American troops in London on leave and with all soldiers recuperating from their wounds. When the air raid warnings sounded the company stayed on stage playing out the scene, only going down to the basement bomb shelter when the very last invalid soldier had been safely escorted out. Sometimes, after the 'All Clear', they would pick up the scene where they had left off.

Father, by 1943, had been stripped of his rank and sentenced to work as a hospital orderly. He was permitted to come home on weekends, but it can't have been easy for him or Mother at home. With the war over, the returning soldiers and the terrible news of the concentration camps was all people could think about. Father took advantage of the general pandemonium and disappeared. I doubt if the authorities even missed him.

I was never to see him again.

In 1986, Mother, Susannah and I went to The Duke of York's to see Stepping Out. *We were seated in the stalls. During the first act Mother began to snuffle. Soon her snuffles turned to sobs and we had to hush her. During intermission, Susannah said, 'Whatever is the matter?'*

'Oh, dear,' Mother snuffled, 'I was remembering that this is where it all began – up there on the stage. That's where dear Paddy and I had our reception and then later we had you two. Oh dear.'

And she wiped her eyes and blew her nose. It was the only time that Mother showed us any emotion about Father.

After *Junior Miss* finished the London run and its subsequent tour of the provinces, Mother had a difficult time finding work. She blamed Father and the fall-out from the negative publicity for her lack of job offers, but in all probability it was because at thirty-five she had finally become too old to play teenagers and she now had to start auditioning for older character roles. She had never been considered a leading lady:

'Much too short!' was the usual gruff response at auditions. This was another bitter pill to swallow.

Her husband having left home never to return, and with well-paying acting jobs harder and harder to find, Mother had to cut her expenses. She let Nanny go. Tiger was sent to live with her sister Audrey in Berkshire. She rented the top two floors of Number 36 and lived in the basement with her old St. Helen's school chum Avril Wood, a daughter of Sir Henry Wood conductor of the Promenade Concerts.

What should she do with us? She was determined to continue acting. *All her life, her career would come first.*

In June 1945, she landed the role of Janey Jenkins, a sluttish young woman, in *The Cure for Love* with Robert Donat. In 1946, after a mercifully brief run in *G.I. Brides at Sea*, she was cast as the cheerful maid, Doto, in Christopher Fry's witty, three-character verse play *A Phoenix Too Frequent* with Paul Scofield and Hermione Hannen. Unable to afford child-care, she *had to do something with us.*

I have a memory from this time. I am three and a half. Mother had been invited to a cocktail party at the home of another old school friend, Denise Farquharson, who had recently married a handsome American Captain. Without a nanny, Mother has had to bring Susannah and me with her. After looking at knees, eating strange little bits of food and drinking too much American soda pop, I needed to pee. Mother tells Susannah to take me to the loo. Once there, my big sister undresses me – completely – and then tries to heft me up onto the lavatory seat. She can't. I'm too heavy. She tells me to go and ask for help. I trundle down the hallway, stark naked except for my white socks and my black patent leather party shoes. To the handsome American Captain, (who I was to come to know later in the States as Federal Judge Frederick van Pelt Bryan), I say, 'Please may I have a potty, 'cos I can't reach the seat.' Then I just remember lots of laughter.

After a stay with our grandparents at their sixteenth century Berkshire cottage in South Moreton, Mother sent us to Hampshire to board with yet another school friend, Violet Slade-Jones, for a few months. Sea Pines at Milford-on-Sea was a wonderful place, a gracious house with large gardens across the road from the beach and the Solent. Violet and

Mother had remained close since their days at St. Helens. 'Auntie' Vi was a lovely woman, tall, graceful and soft-spoken. She and her friend Chris Clark, having both lost their fiancés during the War, had recently opened Sea Pines as a holiday home for children. It was a place where parents could leave their offspring in the long summer holidays, without a worry, while they *did* the Continent. A genteel summer camp across from the Isle of Wight, most children came to stay between May and October. After that the two ladies had the house to themselves. They ran Sea Pines for many years and when they retired they lived together for the rest of their lives.

Susannah's and my first visit to Sea Pines was in 1946 while Mother was deciding what to do with us. I don't remember that first time as I was only three, but I went there several times over the years for short stays during the summer holidays, as a non-paying boarder. I was quite happy there.

It was while we were at Sea Pines that Mother heard about the Actors' Orphanage Fund and Silverlands. I am sure this news was heaven-sent. She could place us there and not have to worry. She qualified financially, her husband was as good as dead — after all she had no idea where he was — and, she wasn't earning nearly as much as she had before the War. With us safely away 'at boarding school,' a common guilt-free euphemism used by many Silverlands parents, she was able to pursue her career and take jobs anywhere in England.

While I was living at Silverlands, Mother worked at repertory theatres in Bristol, Birmingham, Salisbury, Dundee and Manchester, as well as in the occasional West End production. Between acting engagements, Mother taught speech and acting both at RADA and the London Central School of Speech and Drama until early 1955 when, at Tyrone Guthrie's suggestion, she immigrated to North America.

Shortly after leaving us on the steps of Silverlands. Mother went into *Flat Spin* at His Majesty's Theatre (later *Her* Majesty's). It got rather poor notices, but on 5 May 1947 *The Times* critic wrote, 'Mr. John Boxer was a delightfully stupid soldier and Miss Joan White the most amiable of stupid ladies.' The same John Boxer was to send his two young sons to Silverlands for a while. Younger than us, they arrived several years later.

By putting Susannah and I in care of the Actors' Orphanage Fund and opting to continue her career unhampered by two small girls, *and* by forbidding our father to see us, our mother effectively orphaned us.

FOUR

'For Children Made Destitute
by the Profession'

OFTEN, WHEN PEOPLE hear the word 'orphanage' they imagine a grim building, something out of Dickens, overcrowded with bare-footed ragamuffins who exist on thin gruel and harsh beatings. Langley Hall (sometimes called Langley Place) and Silverlands, the homes that the Actors' Orphanage Fund ran '*for children made destitute by the profession*' were anything but grim and no child ever went barefoot or hungry, unless they were being disciplined for bad behaviour and thus sent to bed without supper.

This was not necessarily the case during the first decade of the twentieth century at the first home in Croydon, but in those early years the good people who started the Fund had a great deal to learn about overseeing a home for needy children.

Two big-hearted ladies founded the Actors Orphanage Fund in 1896, Mrs. Carson, wife of the publisher of *The Stage*, and Mrs. Compton, mother of novelist Compton MacKenzie and actress Fay Compton. The great actor/manager Sir Henry Irving lent his name as the Fund's first President. Such was Sir Henry's standing as President that after 1901, he had recruited the new Queen Alexandra as well as the Princess of Wales and the Princess Royal as patrons.

During the Victorian era, and before, many children of itinerant actors suffered from neglect and sporadic education. Actors took jobs in repertory theatres throughout Great Britain, wherever they could find work, and their children were dragged along with them. Backstage areas at provincial theatres were often run-down, draughty and unsanitary and the actors' cheap lodgings or *digs* were sometimes worse.

A Committee was formed, made up of prominent British theatre people, and it was decided that the most pressing need was to provide a home for these children: when one or both parents had died; for those homeless children of the stage born out of wedlock; if there was no means of financial support within the family; or if the children were simply not wanted. Soon their criteria included other theatre professionals as well as actors. At Croydon, in the early years of the new century, a Mr. and Mrs. Ansell were hired to take care of the children. The better-off members of the profession presumably provided funds for salaries and upkeep.

At a Committee meeting on Saturday, November 25, 1911 it was resolved that:

> it would be advisable to dispense with the Ansells' services
> as soon as possible as there had been complaints about their
> treatment of the children, including poor food and the
> alleged starvation of some and, for allowing fifteen year old
> girls to roam about Croydon barefoot and without escort.

Mr. Ansell was summoned before the Committee to explain himself. He did not appear.

A report by the Croydon medical officer stated that,

> Out of the thirty-one children weighed, twenty-five were found
> to be below average and two had inexplicable bladder trouble.

The actor-manager Cyril Maude, who had replaced Sir Henry Irving as President of the Fund in 1905 upon Sir Henry's death, convened a special meeting and informed the Ansells that the Committee had lost confidence in them, giving them the option of resigning or being sacked. They resigned.

This action led to the Committee having to take full responsibility for the children in all current and future homes, rather than the sort of franchise agreement that the Ansells had operated under. With this new oversight, life improved for the children.

In 1915, the Orphanage moved to Langley Hall, a country house dating back to 1628 in Buckinghamshire. Here there was more space for the increasing number of children in need. The new President was Gerald du Maurier who had recently succeeded Cyril Maude. Du Maurier was a distinguished Shakespearean actor who had also had much success in the plays of J. M. Barrie: *The Admirable Crichton*, *What Every Woman Knows*, *Dear Brutus*, and most notably in *Peter Pan*, in which he originated the dual roles of Captain Hook and Mr. Darling in 1904, making him popular with very young audiences. *Peter Pan* was to run in revival for years at Violet Melnotte's new theatre and it helped to put The Duke of York's (later to be my father's theatre) firmly on the map. Under du Maurier, life at Langley Hall improved for the children – somewhat.

In the summer of 1931 Dan Taylor, aged five, went to Langley Hall with his nine-year-old sister Yettey. Dan remembered Langley in an essay he wrote for It's Behind You Dot Com, The Panto Pages.

> The school was divided into two sections – the boys' end that housed the older lads, and the girls' end which included the very youngest boys, like myself, when they first arrived at Langley Hall. The school grounds were very well kept and boasted a cricket pitch, two soccer pitches, two tennis courts and a gymnasium that had fine stage facilities.
>
> The highlight of the Christmas season was our traditional pantomime or 'Panto' as we called it. Peter Jackson, a professional from London, would script his own version of a popular tale like Cinderella or Robinson Crusoe, and then come down to Langley Hall to cast, produce and direct the musical, which was performed on our gymnasium stage, named 'THE BIJOU THEATRE' for the occasion. Practically the entire student body, about 60 of us, was involved in the production: performing on stage, working backstage, assisting with costumes, props and all other necessities for a presentation of this nature. It played to several full houses at Langley, and on two occasions we did three matinees at The Gaiety Theatre in London with one of the currently popular theatre orchestras in the pit. I loved being part of this. My favourite role was that of the cat in Dick Whittington, the popular fable of the man who rid London of all the rats – the four-legged kind. As his faithful

cat, I didn't have to learn any dialogue, not even a 'meow.' The Pantos remain some of my fondest memories of the Orphanage.

Dan Taylor really was an orphan, although not many of the children were. His father, Dan Rolyat, a popular Music Hall comic and Pantomime dame, had died as the result of an accident on stage when Dan was only a year old. A couple of years later, Dan's mother succumbed to breast cancer.

Granville Bantock, nephew and namesake of the composer, had arrived the year before Dan with his older brother Paul. In his own self-published memoir *Lucky Orphan*, Granville writes,

> Langley Hall was a fine old building built in 1628 and
> added to later on. There were many other buildings on the
> grounds. The educational and living arrangements were
> strictly segregated, even at mealtimes. The boys' end of the
> grounds also included a large kitchen garden and orchard and
> was separated from the girls by a high brick wall and metal
> railings. The boys had two classrooms and two dormitories
> each divided into two age groups six to eleven and twelve
> to sixteen. The girls were divided in the same way.

Boys and girls at the Actors' Orphanage usually were between the ages of five and sixteen but, and it was so in my time too, many children arriving as young as two years old. Granville, like myself, was only four years old. Some were even babes-in-arms who had been put into foster care at the Actors' Church Union or Doctor Bernardo's homes before going on to the Orphanage. The Orphanage provided a warm bed, food and education. Until the early 1950's, when the welfare state began subsidising unemployed actors with the dole, between fifty and seventy children were under the Orphanage's care.

In those early years, discipline at Langley was fairly harsh with cold baths and canings a frequent occurrence. Here's Dan again:

> They made sure we understood and followed the rules: staying 'in
> bounds' at all times; having our beds made tidily each morning;
> eating everything on your plate and sitting at table until you did

so; no misuse of any school property; no talking back to anyone in authority; no talking after lights out and many other 'no's'.

When I moved up to the boys end, the Cold Bath was part of the regular school routine at that time. This barbarous practise took place every morning after rising. A bathtub was filled with cold water – very cold water – and you had to take a push-up stance in the tub, then immerse yourself completely. On those first few mornings, our grinning seniors would be stationed around the tub and as we completed our doleful dip and started to get back to dry land, one of them would say You didn't get your head wet – do it again!' When you did it again a hand would hold your head under water for a couple of extra seconds. This went on for several days until we showed we could take it and then the seniors lost interest.

Caning was prevalent in many English schools and probably all boarding schools, but 'Moggy' (Mr. Mowforth the headmaster) kept himself in peak physical condition swinging that cane at us! Seems we spent half our time lined up outside his office door, waiting to get 'six of the best.' If they weren't the best, they were pretty darn good. And they were administered for the slightest infraction of the rules!

Gerald du Maurier died in April 1934, and sweeping changes began to happen at Langley Hall. Noël Coward accepted the presidency of the Actors Orphanage and he would take a much more active role than his predecessors. Immediately, the buildings were redecorated, the railings and gates painted in red oxide. A new boys' dormitory was constructed with more windows and a single bed for each boy – no more bunks. He also introduced a much more lavish Christmas, negotiating free gifts of cakes, fruit, cream, poultry, crackers and sweets for the children. Granville, remembering seeing Coward for the first time, wrote:

I vividly remember Noël Coward's first visit to the orphanage to see the children. He came into our playroom with a box of Mars bars, one for each of us. We couldn't believe it – it would have taken us a whole month's pocket money to buy one. He spoke to us and then sat down at our very old honky-tonk piano and played – it sounded terrific. He came to see us whenever he could, sometimes accompanied by very glamorous ladies. He once came with Ivor Novello and three lovely ladies of the stage in beautiful dresses and large hats – Evelyn Laye, Diana Wynyard and Mary Ellis.

Noël Coward took the Orphanage out of the dark ages. Many of the children had come from terrible poverty and neglect. Langley Hall gave them security and a sense of home and family, but there had still been a slightly Dickensian feeling to the place. Granville, Hugo Bergstrom and Roy Williams, all at Langley before World War Two, agreed with Dan and said cold baths, hard work and regular punishment were the rule of the day until Coward took over.

When Coward came on the scene, Mr. Mowforth the headmaster had been there for quite some time, ruling with his cane. Just before one of Coward's visits, Mowforth had given some young offenders an unusually cruel two dozen lashes each. All the children had rioted, protesting loudly and tearing up property. Coward, on hearing about it, came down immediately from London. He was horrified to discover that this man had been given free rein to run the place – not accountable to anyone. Mowforth was immediately fired and the chief rioters given a talking-to. Coward immediately set about making changes and became an outspoken champion for the children.

With Noël Coward at the helm, the Orphanage became co-educational in all ways. Before, if a boy was seen even looking at a girl he could be punished. At that time, very few orphanages and private schools mixed the sexes. It was very daring, but Coward thought it was the healthy approach, so classes and other activities were now held for boys and girls together. Coward introduced school uniforms and field trips to London theatres; the food improved and kinder staff members were hired. Coward took an active role in each child's development.

At Langley the boys played cricket in the summer. Begun in the nineteen twenties, the cricket team was coached by George Hurst, a retired batsman from Yorkshire. Granville told me that one of the Langley boys, Jack Young, went on to play for Middlesex and England. The team played other area schools including nearby Eton College. Granville remembers,

> I was in the cricket team that played at Eton in 1935 and I will always remember it because of the marvelous tea they gave us afterwards. I had never seen a spread like it, but of course *they* ate that way all the time. What on earth, we wondered, did they eat for dinner? Although the boys on the teams were the same age, the Eton boys were at least six inches taller than us.
>
> Another highlight of the summer cricket was the match against the Actors' Eleven. Frank Lawton, an old boy, would bring along a team of fellow actors, but best of all he would bring his wife, Evelyn Laye. She was so very beautiful and I would follow her everywhere. She would organize the teas in the marquee, helped by dozens of ladies from the London stage. It was one huge party for all those connected with the theatrical profession who had given their time and money for the benefit of the Orphanage. It was a glorious day in the calendar with actresses everywhere in summer dresses and, of course, 'leather on willow.' I especially enjoyed Rex Harrison and Hugh Williams asking me to bowl to them in the nets, but best of all was Evelyn Laye serving tea.

Dan Taylor's recollection of the annual Actors' Match was,

> Autograph hunters had a great workout. Noël Coward was always on hand for the festivities, though he never donned the cricket 'whites,' he was always a very suave host for the event.
>
> It was while Coward was President in 1938 that, after twenty-three years as the Actors Orphanage, Langley Hall was sold and Silverlands, near the Surrey town of Chertsey, was purchased as a more suitable home for the children.

Silverlands was a handsome Georgian mansion just south of London, in what used to be known as the Green Belt, and a mile from Chertsey station where the trains ran regularly from Waterloo. Before the war, school classes continued to be held at the Orphanage in rooms around the outer courtyard. On Sundays, the children walked to Trinity Church in the nearby village of Lyne.

In 1939 the war came and, with German bombers flying overhead and the whole country braced for an invasion, arrangements were made by Noël Coward to evacuate all children between five and fifteen to America. Silverlands had been requisitioned as a convalescent home for wounded soldiers as it was convenient to the newly established St. Peter's war hospital nearby on the Guildford Road.

Initially it was planned that the children would go to Hollywood where members of the British acting community had been persuaded by Noël Coward to help in any way they could. In September 1940, fifty-four children and two staff members sailed on *The Empress of Australia* from Glasgow to Newfoundland. When they arrived in America plans had changed, Hollywood was no longer an option and so they went by train to New York City instead. For the next few years the Edwin Gould Foundation, in Pelham just north of Manhattan, housed them. Because of the United States Immigration restrictions, each of the fifty-four children had to have his or her own sponsor. It was then that the Hollywood community came through. Dame May Whitty was Granville's sponsor:

> Not long after arriving at the (Gould) Foundation I received a letter from Hollywood, it was from Dame May Whitty saying that it would be impossible for her to travel to New York to see me. Instead she had asked her daughter, Margaret Webster to act for her. Margaret Webster, a theatrical producer, lived in New York where she was very involved with the Shakespeare Company. The list of our Hollywood sponsors included most of the British actors and actresses living in California, and they would visit us whenever they were in New York. Charlie Chaplin came several times and so did Cary Grant and Douglas Fairbanks, but when Joan Fontaine visited I fell madly in love in spite of her husband Brian Aherne coming with her. We had hoped to see Noël Coward, but we knew he was acting as an unofficial roving ambassador for Britain and traveling all over the world.

In 1946, the war was over and Silverlands again became home to the returning evacuees and to a new crop of "orphans." How many children who had returned from America were living at Silverlands when I arrived, I don't know? They would have been much older than me and I don't remember them.

Granville had had to return to England during the war. His older brother Paul had joined the air force and had been shot down in 1942. (Several other Orphanage boys gave their lives in World War II.) At his mother's urging but with the Committee's strong reservations, Granville was sent back to war-torn England and at seventeen enlisted in the army. He was stationed in Burma after V-J Day when captured and emaciated Allied soldiers were released from the Japanese camps. On his return to England he met up with another former orphan, Brenda Lordan and in 1952 they were married in Trinity Church, Lyne.

Several of the older children stayed in America. A family from Rockford, Illinois adopted Dan Taylor. Through them and the generosity of others, Dan went to Wesleyan University and eventually landed a job with CBS-TV, got married and raised his family in America. As did I, Dan took his adult children back to England to revisit his childhood home. Back in America, at his home on the Hudson River just an hour or so from where both Liz and I lived, he wrote this:

> A really welcome surprise recently was a letter, followed by a phone call from Lenny Mann, who I have not seen in over sixty years. Within a few seconds, we were chatting away as if we were picking up a conversation we had started in 1943 at the Gould Foundation. Nothing quite compares with moments like these. It was Lenny who suggested that some of us put down on paper remembrances of our Orphanage life and of the adult years that followed. Did the first, in any substantial way, influence the second?
>
> Without the slightest hesitation, the answer from me is an unqualified 'YES.' At the age of five I had no parents. But at Langley Hall, I came to realize that I did have a family – a family of friends who shared the same advantages and disadvantages as I, who were going through the same good

and bad times, the chuckles and the canings, the delights and disappointments. There was always someone to share the best and help you through the worst. To this day, the most important items in life to me are a close-knit family and friends. This I learned at the Actors' Orphanage.

Liz and I had arranged to get together with Dan, but it was not to be. Sadly Dan Taylor passed away on Christmas Day 2006. I was born seventeen years later than he, and our experiences of life at the Actors' Orphanage were somewhat different, but I would add my unqualified 'Yes' to his. It was through the Orphanage that I learned the importance of home and family. I had some fifty siblings and my home was Silverlands.

FIVE

A Stately Home of England

SILVERLANDS, WHEN I lived there, was surrounded by thirty-six acres of open fields and woodlands. A local brewer, with the most fitting name of Robert Porter, built the house in 1814. In 1825, Vice Admiral Sir Henry Hotham, a national hero who had commanded the naval stockade during the Napoleonic wars, and who later accompanied Napoleon when he demanded political asylum and thus was in command of his transport to exile on St. Helena. He retired to England and bought the house as a home for his family. The name *Silverlond*, describing the lovely landscape, was entered in the Chertsey town records as far back as 1420. The twenty-seven thousand square foot mansion with its elegant silvery stone façade, tall sash windows, countless chimneys and broad aspect seemed an unlikely home for a bunch of actors' orphans, but we made it ours.

The main gate to Silverlands still stands at the top of Holloway Hill, a narrow, tree-lined way, off the Guildford Road, just a mile south of Chertsey town. Coming home from school alone after four o'clock in the winter months was terrifying. A lone raised footpath ran along the roadway, which was shrouded on both sides by dense, menacing trees. Sometimes men in cars lurked there. After dark, the 'cats-eyes' in the middle of the road glinted in the lights of passing cars and bicycles adding to the eeriness. Botleys Insane Asylum was, at that time, opposite the Silverlands back gate where the road forked to Longcross on the left and on the right to the nearby village of Lyne.

The front gate was a gate of palatial proportions: wrought-iron palings separated four high stone columns, each one topped by an enormous stone ball. Inside the gate, and set back from the drive, was the Lodge, a small stone house where employees sometimes lived. When empty it became a hide-out for a succession of children. Here, and in other secret places, we tried smoking; fashioning cigarettes out of crushed, dried, possibly poisonous, autumn leaves rolled up in exercise book paper and sealed with Sello-tape. Sometimes the boys used their pocket money to buy real, and equally vile, cigarettes – unfiltered Weights or Woodbines. *It makes me cough to think about that now.*

Once through the gates and past the Lodge, way off to the left stood the house, proudly set on a rise and fronted by a wide grassy expanse interrupted by old trees – which we climbed, a clump of tall plumed pampas grass and two huge rhododendron bushes – in which we made our camps. The approach was a pitted, potholed, curving drive about a quarter of a mile long, but it seemed so much longer to my short legs. To the right were irregular shaped fields and a small copse of silver birch and oak trees. Next to the copse stood an old hut used by our Boy Scout troop, that is until three brothers burned it down in the late nineteen forties. Those three brothers were at Silverlands only briefly and were gone, quite suddenly, after the fire.

Beyond the fields lay the 'Big Woods.' A local man owned these, but he was kind and let us play in them. There we had endless adventures in our secret camps and tree forts, playing Cowboys and Indians and Robin Hood, (girls had to play squaws and Maid Marians) and we always found plenty of wild nuts and berries to sustain us between meals.

All over the grounds grew every kind of wildflower; daisies for our daisy chains, cowslips, Queen Anne's lace, violets, buttercups (which you held under your chin to see if you liked butter), dandelions with their global clocks of seeds for telling the most inaccurate time, and clover from whose flowerets we could suck a smidgeon of nectar while searching for those with the lucky, but elusive, four-leaves. A large and nasty patch of stinging nettles awaited those who took the drive's curve too fast on our bikes. Many a child would hit a pothole and, flying over the handlebars, land in the nettle bed. Covered with blisters, that no amount of rubbing with burdock leaves would alleviate, we were sore for days. Past the nettles was the football field also the cricket pitch, where the boys played with, and against, the local lads. We girls cheered them on from the sidelines and in clement weather we all practiced various forms of outdoor physical activities, depending on who the housemaster was at the time. They came and went.

Further on, the driveway branched left to circle in front of the imposing front door. Here the taxis came from Chertsey Station bringing new children accompanied by anxious, weeping or stoic parents. Some of those same parents would later return to take their children out for tea on Visiting Sunday – always the third Sunday of each month.

To the right, a short, paved lane led down to the woods. We called it Chestnut Avenue because long ago some forward-thinking landscaper had planted a row of horse chestnut trees on either side of it. In the spring, these chestnut trees with their alternating blossoms of pink and white panicles were glorious: in the autumn they gave us 'conkers' for our vicious little games and their sturdy low-hanging branches provided us with many places to hide.

We had races down Chestnut Avenue, at first on sticks with bits of string for reins, which we pretended were hobbyhorses. Later on, we careened down on the brakeless, green, women's Army bicycles we'd been given to share. Chestnut Avenue ended at an old wooden five-bar gate. From there a wide path led through the woods to Lyne. A hundred years before, the Hotham family had driven their carriages along that path on Sundays to worship at Trinity Church. Some of the kids used this short cut on Saturdays after chores were over, with a little square ration coupon in hand, to spend their pocket money on comic books and sweets at the Lyne village shop. Rationing didn't end until I was ten in 1953. Even though the way through the woods was fairly wide, it was a scary walk past those big old trees and, usually, I chose the long way round to Lyne.

Passing Chestnut Avenue, the drive continued, rutted and weedy, past the back entrance and more reminders of past grandeur, with the sentinel owls standing on the gateposts leading to the outer and inner courtyards and the former stables. Outside the gateway were huge piles of coke, which the older boys shoveled into wheelbarrows, trundled them into the inner courtyard and emptied them down the "coke-hole" into the furnace room, every Saturday morning.

Terry told me that when he was on Coke Squad with Carl or Gerry things moved right along: they just tipped the coke into the hole until the pile reached the top. But when he was on with Chris, conscientious Chris would keep going down to the furnace room below to rake the pile out flat. Being put on the Coke Squad with Chris took much, much longer.

Once past that coke pile, the driveway, now the back drive as opposed to the front drive, went down hill from there. Sloping down on the left side was a long grassy slope. Later the chickens of Mr. Fraser's time lived on that hillside and, when they were no more, either eaten or gone, Mr. Slater created a playground of sorts. He put up swings for the little kids and created a sandpit, – really just a hole dug into the hillside with a little sand mixed in. Assorted pieces of junk accumulated there, – old bedsteads and tin cans – which the enterprising little ones turned into creative playthings. Long before the sandpit, when I was one of the little kids, we had our first and only English snowfall. It covered the hillside with barely an inch, but every child grabbed trays, bits of cardboard or just sat on their bottoms and slid down that hill until what little snow there had been was gone. *I would remember that day every time my husband and I took our daughters tobogganing in a two-foot deep New England snowfall.*

The drive continued down past a once glorious, now overgrown, sunken garden where lupines, delphiniums, hollyhocks and other valiant perennials still grew among the weeds; past the undulating asphalt of the old tennis court with its once elegant, small pavilion; past the stand of bamboo where we cut our switches for our punishments; and on the other side of the drive, past the kitchen gardens and small orchard lovingly cultivated by Mr. Hazell. The last bit of land, before the wooden gate onto Lyne Lane, was rented to a local farmer. He kept pigs there and some farm machinery. We used to love to hang over the sties and count the new pink piglets suckling all in a row under their enormous, exhausted mothers.

Between the front and back gateways to Silverlands, at the top of Holloway Hill, was a small bungalow with a big heart. This was the home of Mr. and Mrs. Bert Hazell. Mr. Hazell was in charge of everything to do with the grounds at Silverlands. Helped by the older boys, chiefly by Brian, he planted the kitchen gardens, pruned the trees, mended the fences and mowed the fields.

Mrs. Hazell took in the littlest boys until they were four or five and ready for the big house. She had four children of her own and her house wasn't very big, but she fostered a continuous procession of small Silverlands' boys. No girls were ever put into her care, although some of us were certainly young enough, but we were always welcome to stop by for a cuddle and a sweet. Brian, evacuated from Nazi-occupied Guernsey at two, had stayed with the Hazells during the war and Ken, Stephen, Jonny and Nicky all passed through her capable and loving hands.

The Hazells' garden had an abundance of flowers and vegetables each season of the year. Rose bushes and tall hollyhocks leaned up against the house, as if drawing strength from it. Soldiers and sailors, primroses and forget-me-nots lined the paths in spring. Later came marigolds, snapdragons, love-in-a-mist and more, in a riot of colour all summer and autumn. Tomato plants, big green cabbages, carrots and beets grew alongside tall pea and bean trellises, and the squash plants covered the ground with their trailing vines. The occasional barrow-sized marrow lay supine until Mr. Hazell was ready to enter it in the Chertsey Agricultural Association Fair and win an inevitable prize. It was a family sized garden, everything growing and jumbled together happily, just like the Hazell family; unlike the regimented rows and rows of vegetables that Bert Hazell tended for the big house. *I'm sure my love of gardening began at the Hazells' bungalow.*

When I was older, I became particularly fond of the Hazells' goats. Every day, on my way to Sir William Perkins' Grammar School, where I went after I turned eleven, I would walk past those goats, my bulging satchel slung over my shoulders (I always had much too much homework at Perkins). One day, a page of my homework blew into the goats' enclosure. The nearest billy goat promptly ate it. He seemed to enjoy my arithmetic homework much more than I did. From then on my math teacher, Miss Gerrish, seemed to believe 'the goat ate my homework' excuse, every time. She was either gullible or perhaps she just didn't care.

Next to the Hazells' garden was a small growth of trees known to us all as the Hazell Woods. They were much less intimidating than the Big Woods but in the Hazell Woods there was a very long and large mound of earth covered in moss, roots and stones. We would tiptoe around it because we had been told, by the big kids of course, that a giant lay sleeping there and if we woke him up, he would eat us. That was the stuff of nightmares when I was small.

At the edge of these woods stood a very tall beech tree. We called it the Alarm Tree because it had lots of horizontal branches, making it easy to climb to the very top. From there you could see for miles and give the alarm if trouble, like a master, was coming our way.

One day, we younger ones were all climbing this tree; Carl, Kenny, Sue, Michael, Caroline, Liz and me. Liz was at the top and suddenly she fell, all the way down. She bounced off what seemed like every single branch. But she didn't scream, she squealed. We all scrambled down as fast as we could, fearing the worst. But Liz wasn't dead, she wasn't even unconscious, she was just mad as a hornet. A wicked gash had ripped open the back of her thigh where a branch had broken and caught her. I went with her as she limped, trudged and grumbled up to the house. Matron called the doctor in from the hospital across the road.

He said, "Young lady, you need stitches."

Liz yelled and screamed, "I don't want stitches"

The doctor got mad at her and went back St. Peter's. So Liz had no stitches, just salt and a big piece of sticking plaster. We all went back to climbing trees. *Liz still has the scar.*

We had lots of trees to climb and bushes to hide in. We made camps inside the two rhododendron bushes with the huge purple and white blossoms on the east side of the house. Once inside the staff wouldn't know where we were, or so we thought, and we could be within the sound of the bell or the gong when told, 'Now children, don't go too far away, it's almost supper time.' It was in those rhododendron bushes that Sue and Michael were caught showing each other their 'charms'. We all showed each other what we had back then and nobody got too excited about it. Sue and Michael were the only ones who actually got caught.

I had a special place that I called the umbrella tree. It was quite short with branches that fell from the top touching the ground all the way around in a circle, forming a sort of tent. In there, I could hide and get away from everyone, be invisible and get lost in a book. There were lots of trees and bushes, nooks and crannies to hide in if you didn't want to join in the endless games.

The house itself was stately and grand. To a small, chubby four year-old it was enormous, and even revisited later after years of wear and tear, its land sold-off to a nursery farmer, the house maintained a regal, landed-gentry look. It was, in retrospect, an unlikely place to house a bunch of ragged children. Its very name, Silverlands, conjures up a sweeping estate and rich living. But reality and income tax had made it too difficult to maintain as a private, one-family home and so, like many other more stately mansions, it lowered its standards and took in children.

Ray wrote recently from his home in far away Tasmania,

> Silverlands, Holloway Hill, Chertsey, Surrey – that was the address I remembered so well (at the top of so many unanswered letters to my mother). I can recall every inch of the old place. It is not unusual for me to close my eyes and wander to any part of the building I choose. It is so real I could draw it. I remember where I carved my initials under the great oak staircase in the entrance hall, where I hid small treasures, maybe a packet of sweets or a stick of Palm Toffee in one of the many tunnels below the kitchen. I learnt to kick a football between the air raid shelters next to the small hill where we played "kick the can" – I can remember faces and still put names to them. I remember *all* the favorite places to play – especially the Big Woods.

The exterior façade was of silver-gray stone with clean lines, imposing sash windows and many entrances and exits, all of which we used to the fullest when escaping our taskmasters. Not counting the labyrinthine basement, the main house had three stories. The ground floor rooms had very high ceilings, polished parquet floors, carved wooden paneling on the doors and ornate plaster molding all over the ceiling and walls. The second floor front was equally grand with large sunny bedrooms and the same ornate plaster moldings and parquet flooring. Here the ceilings were not quite so high and the parquet, not quite so parquet. We girls eventually slept four or more to a room, where just one four-poster bed used to be.

Another wing of first floor bedrooms, called 'the bachelor quarters' in days gone by, was above the kitchens and overlooked the courtyard and the front entrance, These were not so grand and were given over to the boys in my early years before 'family groups' were introduced. The staff, except for Matron, the housemaster and the Headmaster's family, lived on the top floor under the great lead-covered roof. Matron lived in the girls' wing. The current housemaster lived in the boy's wing and the Headmaster had a small suite of rooms above the boys' wing and the front hall. This later became the sickroom and dispensary in Miss Rennie's days, and finally the Slaters' flat.

The massive double front doors opened into an entry foyer with a black and white marble floor and recessed side windows. On each windowsill sat a relic from bygone days at Langley Hall. On one stood a bronze bust of Sir Gerald du Maurier with his long patrician nose and his oh-so-cavernous nostrils, so convenient for little fingers. Across from him in a tall glass case, stood a cricket bat – a very special cricket bat once owned by Sir Jack Hobbs, England's premier batsman for nearly thirty years. I didn't know that back then. Perhaps he had played cricket at Langley in Frank Lawton's Actors' Match once. He had signed it on the flat side of the blade. You could swivel the bat by the handle protruding through the top of the case. I was to know these memorials well over the years because, once old enough, Janet and I dusted and polished the front hall, Sir Gerald's head and Sir Jack's cricket bat, every Saturday morning.

The foyer led into the grand front hall. Heavily paneled in oak and richly carved with wreaths of foliage and fruit, several Ionic-style oak columns held up an equally ornate ceiling. *To think we grew up oblivious of these architectural details.* A grand staircase, equally rich in carvings, led to the front bedrooms. The stairway was wide and high. On either side smooth wooden banisters, perfect for sliding down, stopped at a square landing and divided, ending with fruited newel posts. At the top of the staircase, the stairwell was surrounded with an ornate wooden balustrade over which some older boys had hung the Sneak's Chair.

The telephone lived all by itself in a cupboard under the stairs, Chertsey double three six eight, opposite the entrance to the boys' wing. It was in this cupboard that we received calls from our parent – either to say they would be coming on Sunday, or they would not be coming. It was not, for me, a particularly happy cupboard.

Each Christmas, a large fir tree was set up on the square landing and Father Christmas, in a long red robe, cotton wool beard and shoes suspiciously like the current headmaster's, came down the stairs from above and ceremoniously handed each of us two envelopes before giving out any packages. These were postal orders for five shillings (later ten): one from the President (Noël Coward, later Laurence Olivier), and one from the Committee, both of which we duly put into our post office savings books.

The marble fireplace was so big that three six year olds could stand up inside it. I once overheard two visitors remarking,

"Lovely fireplace isn't it? Adam, I think."

From then on, to me, that fireplace was called Adam. Over the mantel hung a large framed photograph of His Majesty, King George VI (replaced in 1952 by Her Majesty Queen Elizabeth II, first in her coronation dress and later in a twin-set and pearls with her corgis). Another smaller fireplace across from "Adam" stood just by the foyer door, where a Victorian gentleman might warm his hands after a cold winter carriage ride.

There was a wide multi-paned window with a cushioned seat that overlooked the front driveway. From there we watched, in anticipation, for the arrival of our relatives on Visiting Sundays – those of us with relatives who came.

From the front hall, another set of double doors led to the main part of the house. To the right of these hung the portrait of the actor William Terriss, his eyes following us as we passed him. Through these doors, a wide corridor ran the length of the house on one side of which were windows that looked out onto the inner courtyard and the kitchens and sculleries below.

On the other side of the corridor, massive doors led into the various main rooms. The first door opened into the assembly room. This had once been the Hothams' double drawing room with baroque plaster mouldings on the walls and the high ceiling with ornate cornicing. It had an intricate parquet floor, carved niches for long-gone statuary, a marble over-mantle, huge inset mirrors and four seven-foot-high windows that looked east to the countryside beyond. French doors led out to the terrace. It was a magnificent room. In Queen Victoria's time, the family used this room for grand balls. We kept that tradition going by having dancing lessons in there and the occasional fancy dress "hop."

In 1982, my first marriage had just ended. Ed, who had been one of the older boys at Silverlands and lived in Canada, came down to visit me in the States and bring me courage (most of us have been through at least one divorce). I took him on a tour of Edith Wharton's house, The Mount, in Lenox, Massachusetts where I worked as publicist for both the house and the resident Shakespearean theatre company. As we walked through the main rooms of Wharton's grand home, Ed said,

'Judy, how can you work here? Look at the mouldings! Look at the floors! Look at the doors and windows! It's just like Silverlands.'

'I'm used to it.' I said, 'Anyway, my office is up under the roof, in the servant's quarters.'

Next door to the Assembly room was the dining room, large enough to seat all fifty of us at one sitting at the long, green, easy-to-clean, Formica-topped tables. An enormous metal hot plate, blocking the original fireplace, dominated the room. Early on we queued up like Oliver Twist for our daily rations of porridge at breakfast or over-cooked vegetables with grey meat or boiled cod at supper. Two doors led off the main corridor into this dining room. Across the hall was the pantry with a double sink and big dish drainers where we took turns doing the washing up. A small service lift in the pantry brought the food up from the kitchens below. In the hallway stood the gong, which summoned us twice a day (three times on weekends and holidays) to meals.

Beside the hot plate a connecting door led into what had once been the morning room. (All the formal rooms had connecting doors). It had big sunny, south-facing windows and French doors leading to the outside. When I was small only the staff used it. Later it was where we played games: Monopoly, Ludo, Wembley, Tiddley Winks, Pick-Up Sticks, chess and checkers. On Christmas Day, we gathered in here after church and a special midday meal, to listen to the King's (later the Queen's), speech on the wireless.

Next to this room was the loggia, a marble-floored sun-porch draped in old wisteria vines. It looked past the ugly air raid shelters, built during the war for the nurses and recuperating soldiers. When the Langley Hall kids arrived at Silverlands in 1938 there were no air raid shelters, just a wide expanse of lawn leading down in a series of grassy slopes through the trees to the sunken garden and tennis court. The air raid shelters were ugly, unfriendly buildings and quite discordant with the beauty of the house. Two rectangular red brick boxes with thick, black-tarred roofs; a narrow, freestanding brick wall stood a couple of feet from each open entry. Inside them, it was musty and damp, full of crawling beetles, worms and wood lice. A long, cold, wide concrete ledge for seating ran along each inner wall, narrow apertures provided the only ventilation. If a bomb had made a direct hit, I'm sure everyone inside would have been squashed flat as pancakes. They quite ruined the view from the loggia.

The headmaster's office was on the other side of the loggia. A warm wood-paneled study, it was a room we only ever entered to be repri-manded or to meet with the Committee ladies and gentlemen on their regular visits. Here the boys bent over awaiting the slipper, the strap or the cane on their raised and quivering bottoms. A fireplace in the office was where a coal fire burned on winter days to keep the headmaster warm. All of the grander rooms had fireplaces, most of which were never used. Radiators heated the rest of the house, sparsely, fired up by the enormous boilers in the nether regions, stoked with the coke shoveled by the big boys on Saturday mornings.

A narrow corridor, alongside the office, led to the recreation room and library. Once upon a time, the 'Rec' room (later known as the 'noisy room' by our nicer staff) and the library beyond had been one very large, elegantly oak-paneled room. Even in our rambunctious days there re-mained vestiges of its former grandeur, despite the ugly particle- board partition that divided the room. A handsome fireplace shared the chim-ney with the headmaster's office. While there was never a fire in it for the likes of us, above the mantle was a deep alcove in which there was room for three children to sit. In winter, we took turns climbing up to warm our bums from the heat emanating from the office fire. Next to that fireplace was a huge old console radio set that crackled and popped and played Mario Lanza, Frankie Laine, Doris Day and Pat Boone, and later, Tommy Steele, Cliff Richard, Elvis Presley and Lonnie Donegan, if you got the dial just right. The rest of the room was bare, save for a few wooden folding chairs and an old ping-pong table.

A large bay window with high window seats looked out at the air raid shelters and a small hill, which in springtime was covered with daffodils. On the top was a solitary gravestone covered in moss and lichen and engraved with the words "THE OLD MAN – APRIL 1929." Some boy ghoulishly insisted that some old retainer was buried there and his ghost walked the grounds at Halloween. But Brian told me it was the grave of a former owner's favorite horse and that the horse was buried upright – hence the height of the hillock. That horse must have been much loved to have such a profusion of daffodils growing all over his grave.

In the 'Rec' room was a small stage where we sometimes put on plays, but ours were nothing like the Pantos from the Langley Hall days. On rainy days we played ping-pong and British Bulldog, Grandmother's Footsteps and Blind Man's Buff. I hated the dry-mouthed, heart-thumping terror of *Murder in the Dark,* but I dared not show it for the greater fear of being teased. In here, various masters taught us things like Indian club swinging, boxing, intimidation and jitterbugging. A large square, rather dirty skylight allowed light to filter in and also enabled smaller children to watch any teenage *shenanigans* (Miss Rennie's favorite word) from above.

On the other side of the partition was the library. It had beautiful built-in shelves on which sat a sparse collection of donated books, most of them much too boring to read. Both the library and the 'Rec' room had the same ornate carvings and baroque details as the rest of the house. Even the radiator grills were elaborate.

In the library our desks, for homework and Sunday letter writing, were also carved – these with former inmates initials and intricate, ink-filled gouges of cars and the occasional Anglo-Saxon epithet. A fifteen-foot wide by six-foot high window filled the west wall of the library and overlooked the former stables. Several towering chestnut trees, the eating kind, provided us with chestnuts for 'chibby' nights around a bonfire. I was nine and standing by this window staring out at those trees, frozen in a mixture of terror and erotic pleasure as one of the older boys put his hand into my navy blue knickers and massaged my groin. He made me swear never to tell.

I recently came across an old photograph, from the turn of the century, showing a large pipe organ in the middle of this room when it was a forty by thirty foot library with twelve-foot high ceilings, and no unsightly partition. The room is richly furnished with deep leather armchairs and low tables; the shelves are filled with handsome leather-bound volumes.

Outside the 'Rec' room entrance, a rather humble backdoor led out to the inner courtyard under which was the infamous Den of Death. First floor utility rooms looked onto the inner courtyard: a lavatory, a rubbish bin, a broom closet, and the pantry where we washed endless dishes and hauled our daily rations, and occasionally our friends, up from the kitchen on the dumb waiter. An iron fire escape ran down one side of the courtyard, providing an escape route from the boys' quarters. The central back staircase spiraled from the basement to the very top floor. In the shaft was a lift, which was never used and heavily padlocked most of the time. We climbed those stairs every day.

On the first floor landing by the girls' wing was the linen closet and sewing room with our individual laundry baskets. From these our clothing bundles with clean knickers, liberty bodices and second-hand clothes were handed out every Saturday evening, so that we would have clean clothes for the Lord on Sunday – one bundle per child per week. Second-hand clothes were delivered from time to time from charity shops. The older girls' job was to sort the clothing into sizes. These clothes were meant to fit you, not necessarily to suit you.

There were six large and three smaller bedrooms off the long wide central corridor of the girls' wing, each room with ceilings almost as high as those on the main floor. The corridor ran the length of the house and was as inviting as the front hall banisters. We used to tie our pillows around our middles, get a running start at one end of the corridor and slide all the way to the other end. I was about six when my pillow slipped and got a thick four-inch splinter in my tummy, just above my navel. I screamed, but

I got little sympathy from Matron, who just yanked it out and swabbed me with iodine, leaving a bit of wood inside me to fester for a while.

On this floor were two large bathrooms. Each had two old-fashioned hipbaths and one long tub. Once a week was bath night. The hipbaths could hold two small bodies, the big bath three or more in a couple of inches of tepid water. In those early days the water wasn't changed between bodies so it was good to be first for the bath, before the scum built up too much. There were sinks, where we brushed our teeth, and toilets with high cisterns and pull chains.

Up the back stairs on the very top floor in the former servants rooms, now staff bedrooms, was a window or two that opened onto the huge lead roof. When the staff was elsewhere, we used to sneak up and go out on the roof. It was strictly forbidden, because the lead made our clothes filthy *and* it was dangerous, but anything forbidden was fair game.

The main house was built around a central inner courtyard, underneath which were the coal and coke storage cellars, and other dark places. In my early years, I was told, a handyman called Vic lurked down here and 'felt up' the older girls. The basement had cavernous kitchens, sculleries, pantries, laundry rooms and wine cellars. Many were unused, ill lit and scary.

Beyond the inner courtyard, through an archway built to accommodate horse-drawn delivery carts, was the outer courtyard surrounded by the former stables, garages and outside toilets. In the former pre-war classrooms, we did crafts and kept pets, and under a shelter of sorts were bicycle racks for all those green, brakeless, women's ex-Army bicycles, which later were replaced by more presentable and safer ones. Above the archway was where at fifteen I shared a room with Gay and Margaret, 'far from the madding crowd'. The only drawback to our isolation was the bell, which hung in the tower above our heads and was rung, ten minutes before each meal, to summon everyone in from outdoors. The gong, outside the dining room, was rung five minutes later and woebetide the child who came in late and unwashed for meals.

The house itself was a splendid place, architecturally inspiring, challenging to clean – and clean it we girls did every week – and filled with many secret hiding-places. It was where I lived and grew for more than twelve years.

SIX

Noël Coward Raises the Wherewithal

IN 1949, THE Aggitters were dismissed and the bamboo switch-es went with them. A new headmaster and wife team, Mr. and Mrs. Savage-Bailey, came with a kinder attitude, despite their unusual name. Corporal punishment became much more rare. If Mr. Savage-Bailey caught you running in the corridors, he would make you go back and walk slowly, saying, "You'll get there faster if you walk." The Savage-Baileys used a more psychological approach to child rearing, with lots of earnest talk and practical punishments: peeling tons of potatoes or wash-ing dishes after meals for a week. Not that this made much difference to our general behaviour.

Shortly after the Savage-Baileys' arrival, Noël Coward visited Silverlands to meet them. He found them to be kind and in his diary he wrote:

> Thursday, 20 October 1949. I drove to Silverlands. It has been
> repainted and is looking not too bad. The Savage-Baileys seem
> all right. He is obviously a kind man but I fear, on the weak
> side. The children were in wild spirits and I was cheered to
> see they were not looking downtrodden and dismal. I had a
> talk with Savage-Bailey about sex and told him not to get too
> fussed because all children had sex curiosity and too much
> emphasis on its sinfulness would only make it more attractive,
> and that as long as he kept it within bounds he could close
> an eye discreetly every now and then. I am sure this was
> good advice although perhaps not strictly conventional.

Obviously, we had been trying the new headmaster's patience, run-ning wild in our relief at the Aggitters' departure.

Coward's advice to the Savage-Baileys about the sexual curiosity of their fifty or so young charges was probably the very best even though, as he said, it was unconventional. To try and monitor six-year-olds playing doctor and nurse with dolls on the hillside, ten-year-olds exchanging genital views in the rhododendron bushes, twelve-year-old girls having a 'quick feel' in the middle of the night in the boys' bedrooms, or fourteen-year-olds climbing down the ivy to meet undesirable members of the opposite sex in town, would probably have driven the poor man completely round the bend.

Because of the Aggitters' dismissal, Coward ordered that transportation be arranged, at least once a month, for two or three committee members to visit Silverlands and see how things were.

Coward himself visited Silverlands several times when I was a child, sometimes alone arriving with a photographer to snap pictures of him surrounded by us as he played the piano or walked with us all around the grounds. Sometimes, he was accompanied by glamorous figures from the stage and screen. When he visited with Marlene Dietrich, we were all gathered together in front of the loggia and each given a postcard-sized photograph of her (some kids still have that photograph). The two stars sat on the steps in the middle and we were arranged around them, the smallest in front. We were instructed to hold up our pictures of Marlene, with her image towards the camera of course, while the photographer set up his tripod and took several publicity shots for future fund-raising appeals. *Getting all of us to sit still must have tried the patience of a saint.*

Afterwards, wearing lots of pancake make-up, a form-hugging grey suit, a jaunty little hat and very high-heeled shoes, Marlene Dietrich teetered down the pot-holed back drive holding tight to Caroline's hand, to inspect the new piglets in the pigsties. Noël Coward followed with Lally and Margaret on either side of him, the rest of us trooping along behind. On the way back up the drive, Marlene stumbled and turned her elegant ankle, resulting in a slight sprain. Hopping on one foot, she was helped up the driveway by two sturdy boys, until Mr. Coward's motorcar came to the rescue. This, of course, garnered us even more newspaper coverage.

It was during Marlene's visit, before she turned her ankle, that little blond Jonny was told to go upstairs and put his pajamas on – over his clothes – get into bed and wait. It was only about two o'clock in the afternoon! Soon Marlene and Coward came into his bedroom and Marlene snuggled up to the five year old and read him a story in her smoky, German-accented voice while Coward looked on. Photos taken, pajamas off, Jonny was released to go back outside to play some more. He remembers thinking they both smelled of the same perfume.

Coward had also been to visit with the actress and comedienne Gertrude Lawrence when Silverlands re-opened after the war. Miss Lawrence had herself just returned to England after a long stay in the States and was appearing in *September Tide* by Daphne du Maurier on the West End. One of her co-stars was Michael Gough, later of television's *Dr Who* and *Batman* fame. (We learned much later on, when such things were knowable, that Gough had fathered at least two of the children at Silverlands – they were never to learn they were related until it was too late. Several of my fellow orphans had irregular parentage.) Miss Lawrence had done a benefit for 'Noël's children', as she called us, and had come down to visit, but I was too young to remember her.

Coward was president of the Actors' Orphanage Fund from 1934 until 1956. During this time, Coward was well established as both an actor and a playwright. He wrote and starred in *Design for Living, Tonight at 8:30* and *Private Lives* (the last two with Gertrude Lawrence). During the war, he had written the patriotic film *In Which We Serve* and the memorable *Brief Encounter*. After the war, his career continued in film, on the stage and in many nightclub reviews.

When he first took over the presidency, the children were still at Langley Hall. A forward-thinking man for his time, he was disturbed to find that the children were segregated by sex. With Coward at the helm, the Orphanage became co-educational in all ways. Very few orphanages and private schools, at that time, mixed the sexes. What he did was considered very daring then, but Coward thought it was the healthy approach and so most activities were now held for boys and girls together. Coward introduced school uniforms and field trips to London theatres, and staff members with a more modern approach to child rearing were hired.

When reading Philip Hoare's excellent *Noel Coward a biography*, I came across the following declaration on page 259 by Roy Williams, who was at Langley Hall and Silverlands before World War II. Replying as to whether Noel Coward was truly altruistic regarding the Actors' Orphanage, Williams told Hoare he thought it possible that Coward did it in the hope that this would be his contribution to charity and society and that there might be some reward for that, and when he realized that there wasn't going to be any, his interest dropped.

I take great exception to this view! Coward was president for *twenty-two years*, only resigning in 1956 when, because of tax problems, he moved to Jamaica. Until then, he appeared at every annual Theatrical Garden Party, and he brought along his celebrity friends to help raise money. The photographers came to help raise awareness of the Orphanage. *And* Coward took an active role in each child's development.

While he came to visit only when his busy schedule allowed (and he was a very busy man all his life), Lorn Loraine, his secretary and amanuensis, was always involved. She served on the Committee throughout Coward's presidency and beyond. A warm and caring lady with a kind face, she wore her long brown hair pulled back from her face and arranged in a complicated chignon. Mrs. Loraine came down to Silverlands regularly; interested in each individual child, she asked us questions about school and family. Several times I was to meet with her and other Committee members in the headmaster's office. Lorn Loraine, being on Noël Coward's payroll, of course reported her findings to him.

Ken had come to Coward's special attention over a disciplinary matter – perhaps about the Sneak's Chair of which, no doubt, the staff knew.

On 10 July 1950 Coward wrote this entry in his diary:

> Quite a day. Drove with Lornie to Wimbledon to see a possible new house for the orphanage. Not bad. Lunched at The Ace of Spades, then went to see Madge Titheridge ... After this we drove to Silverlands. All the children look healthy, happy and well fed. The problem boy is Peter Collinson, who has been behaving badly and been threatened with expulsion. I took him out and talked to him. He is twelve (*actually Ken was fourteen, born 1 April*

1936} and bright and highly strung. He is being torn to pieces by his divorced parents. He is in an emotional turmoil. I talked to him firmly and made him promise me personally that he would behave well in future and in return I promised him that I would look after him and be his friend. I honestly don't think he will transgress again. Actually he practically broke my heart. I may be over-sentimental but a sensitive little boy bereft of all personal affection is to me one of the most pathetic things in the world.

Ken might well have been in an emotional turmoil about his parents – we all had emotional turmoil about our parents from time to time – but the Ken I remember was our head boy and seemed to be a very cool customer. I suspect that, having being threatened with expulsion, he had used his innate acting talent to play on Coward's sympathy. Ken was actually his middle name; there was another Peter at Silverlands so we knew him as 'Ken'.

As Peter Collinson he became a successful film director. Among his films are Up the Junction, The Long Day's Dying *and* The Italian Job *(1969), in which he directed Noël Coward, Benny Hill and Michael Caine. Coward remained true to his promise and helped Ken/Peter get his first job and a leg up in the entertainment business. Sadly, Ken died of cancer in 1980 at forty-four.*

When we were little, we really had no idea who Noël Coward was. We probably heard that he was in the theatre and so we thought he did the same kind of work as our parents. All I knew was that from time to time this nicely dressed, posh-sounding man came to see us. He would come upon us outside, playing hide-and-seek in and around the air-raid shelters and would call out, 'Hello boys and girls. Having a jolly time are you?'

Or if I, or someone else, was reading on the loggia steps, he would bend down and say, "Hello young lady, what are you reading?"

I, being shy, probably whispered, "*The House at Pooh Corner*" or "*Rupert Bear.*"

It was abundantly clear that he took a genuine interest in us, however, and that we all registered with him as individuals.

Much later, when I was a young actress in New York in 1963, my agent sent me to audition for High Spirits, *the musical version of his play* Blithe Spirit, *which he was to direct. I stood on that Broadway stage, my knees knocking, my heart thumping, staring out into the black hole of the house. Suddenly I heard that unmistakable voice:*

Hello, Judy my dear. How nice to see you again.

You were at Silverlands weren't you? I thought I recognised you.

I hadn't seen him for more than eight years!

As children of the theatre, our principal benefactors were the more established and wealthier members of the profession. They served on the Committee, worked on fund-raising events and, in some cases, donated the proceeds of a current West End matinee to the Actors' Orphanage Fund. The older children ushered for these performances.

Liz and I were small and chunky, bespectacled (me) and missing teeth (she), and we were never singled out for any special occasions. (My golden curls had turned brown and straight by the age of six, although Liz has remained a blonde all her life.) It was always our more adorable siblings who were chosen. In 1949 Susannah, shy sweet Caroline and Desmond, who was short for his age with a cheeky face, went up to London to make a presentation to the Queen (later Queen Mum) at a film festival. Desmond carried a gold key on a cushion and the girls gave her a large bouquet. Liz and I and Desmond's sister Valerie, were allowed to go up to London with them that day, but we had to stand in the rain with Matron, under umbrellas outside Buckingham Palace, and watch as our siblings were driven by in a shiny black Rolls Royce. Caroline and Susannah went to London again, this time with flowers for the Dowager Queen Mary, and Caroline was chosen to present a bouquet, all by herself, to Anna Neagle. Later, while she was living at Rutland Gate in 1952, Susannah presented flowers to Mary Martin and Noël Coward after a benefit for the Orphanage at the Café de Paris. She wore a new rainbow-coloured dress for the occasion made of that new synthetic discovery – nylon.

The principal fund-raising event for Silverlands, and Langley Hall before that, had always been the annual Theatrical Garden Party held at various venues in and around London: in Roehampton and at Queen Mary's Garden in Regent's Park. Lord and Lady Louis Mountbatten, the American movie star Mary Pickford, the Duchess of Kent and many other luminaries had cut the ribbon over the years. Noël Coward and his crew, led by the indefatigable Lorn Loraine, laboured for weeks before these garden parties, lining up the attractions and the star turns, and some of the older children were even chosen to perform. Brian, Desmond and Susannah were on the gymnastics team. Susannah went to at least two of those garden parties with the team. She told me later how they all did back flips and somersaults and then, for the grand finale, formed a pyramid, with Susannah (the smallest) perched on the top, grinning from ear to ear.

What brought the people out in throngs to pay their two shillings and sixes was the opportunity to meet a famous person. Noël Coward alone was probably enough for some autograph hounds, but add Trevor Howard, Greer Garson or Gladys Cooper and you couldn't see the grass for the fans. The Theatrical Garden Parties in the late 1940s brought in about £4,000 each which, after expenses, was probably just enough to pay Silverlands' heating bill.

Coward made a last attempt to raise more money with the Garden Parties. In 1950, he decided to try running the event over two days, giving it a new name: *The Theatre and Film Carnival*. In the souvenir program he wrote:

> Our regular supporters have probably been wondering why
> we decided to run the Theatrical Garden Party, under its
> new guise, the Theatre and Film Carnival, for two days.
> The reason is that this event is the main source of income
> for our work looking after the children of our less fortunate
> colleagues. Costs have risen to such an extent that the amount
> gained by a one-day show is not sufficient for our needs.

He went on to say, if it is a success this year, we hope to do the same thing next year, and for many years to come.

It was not a success. In Coward's own words it was a 'Balls-up'. *The Daily Mail* was sponsoring the event yet gave them no advance publicity. The rest of the press stayed away *because* this was a *Daily Mail* event. The result was a very poor turnout and they made less in two days that they had previously in one.

Coward wrote in his diary:

'Saturday, 3 June. Second day of the Theatre and Film Balls-up. Worked hard from 2 p.m. until 10 p.m. Signed thousands of autographs, sang hundreds of songs, handsomely supported by my dear ones.'

Noël Coward really did care about us and he worked hard to raise the wherewithal for our keep. That two-day affair was the very last Garden Party that Coward organized. In 1951 he, along with theatre producers Charles Russell and Lance Hamilton, put on the first annual *Night of a Hundred Stars* at the London Palladium. In one night, this event made more money than all previous Garden Parties combined. These midnight galas kept us afloat for years.

To help the fundraising along, publicity was needed, and Coward was the principal magnet for that. It usually paid off especially with some of us 'poor little orphans' involved. Just before Susannah left Silverlands for Rutland Gate, she was chosen for a cameo role in the filming of 'Christmas at the Actors' Orphanage', to be aired on the popular BBC television show *In Town Tonight*. Coward went down for the event:

Thursday, 7 December 1950. Lunched with Ann Todd and David Lean. Saw their film of Jamaica, which is lovely. Drove with them down to Silverlands, where a Christmas party was televised; paper caps and crackers and general bonhomie.

Brian Johnston, then an early British television personality who went on to become a popular cricket commentator and something of a national treasure, arrived at the front door dressed as Father Christmas. Susannah was given a limp vegetable and told to say,

"Here's a carrot for Rudolph!"

Kneeling with Liz, Ann and Caroline on the window seat in the front hall, we watched my sister in action. Outside the front door stood a scrawny old horse with deer antlers tied lopsidedly on to its head; attached to its harness was an odd assortment of bells. The local farmer was having a hard time keeping the horse still for the camera.

Noël Coward was right about the paper hats, crackers and bonhomie. We had all been dressed in our Sunday best, with paper hats on our heads, and had gathered in the Assembly room to sing, with Coward at the piano. A staff member's daughter sat on his lap and we hoped she didn't wet her knickers, as she often did. After Father Christmas arrived with that horse and Susannah had said her line, we were all told to sit on the floor in front of the grand front hall staircase. Mr. Johnston, as Father Christmas, handed us each a gaily-wrapped package. We were instructed to make appropriate sounds of delight but not to open the packages. So, as the cameras rolled, we dutifully 'oohed' and 'aahed', and some shook the packages; gaily-wrapped parcels were rare indeed. Alas, those packages were stage props. There was nothing inside them. After the filming was over we had to give them back. It was a big disappointment, but it was *only* the seventh of December.

Actual Christmases at Silverlands were fun. It was a rule that, even if our relatives wanted us to come and see them, we all *had* to stay at Silverlands because there were always those who would never get to go away. Then on Boxing Day, those of us who had somewhere to go were put on the train to visit our families for a few days until school started again in the New Year. But Christmas Day and Christmas Eve were always at Silverlands.

Before Christmas, we went every year to the Panto in nearby Windsor. At matinees we took up several rows in the stalls at the Theatre Royal and from there we noisily hissed the villains and cheered the principal boy. Sometimes there would be other groups of children on the same day we went. Once, I remember, there was a group of children who, in those unenlightened days, were called 'spastics'. Those poor kids were afflicted with involuntary movement and incoherent speech. We, who were so hale and hearty, made fun of them, I am ashamed to say. After that we were all severely reprimanded and reminded of our good fortune and rude health.

Each year, two big motor coaches pulled up to the front door and everyone, staff and kids, got in and went to London to see *Toad of Toad Hall* or *Where the Rainbow Ends*, which I loved. *Where the Rainbow Ends* was about a group of children who get separated from their parents until, helped by Saint George, they find their parents and rescue them. I remember a dragon breathing fire in there somewhere. Apparently, because *Where the Rainbow Ends* was rather too 'rah-rah' about the British Empire, it is now considered politically incorrect; but back then, being kids longing for absent parents, we loved it.

The day before Christmas at Silverlands every year, a huge fir tree was cut down, dragged through the front door by the older boys and housemasters and set up on the bottom landing of the ornate front hall staircase and a big Yule log was put on top of paper and kindling in the front hall fireplace. The older children decorated the tree with real candles in clip-on holders, tinsel and the paper chains that we little ones had all been busily making for days out of coloured paper strips and paste.

On Christmas Eve, in those middle ages when I was seven, eight and nine, the constant four in our dormitory – Liz, Caroline, Janet and I – hung our pillowcases on the ends of our iron bedsteads.

Janet had arrived in early 1952 with her twin brother Bernard. She was rather serious looking until she grinned and in dancing class she proved to be double-jointed. She could bend over backwards and grab her own ankles, flip over backwards and forwards, and bend her thumb back to touch her wrist – very impressive to someone who couldn't even touch her own toes. And she could play the piano by ear!

Anyway, on Christmas eves after lights out, giggling and stubbing our toes, we crept out of bed and staggered about in the dark. An old toy, a special coloured pencil or a dog-eared book, each carefully wrapped, was pulled out from under our lumpy, horsehair mattresses and put into the pillowcase 'stockings'. We had each received those presents from one of our room-mates, in much the same way, the year before and so it was crucially important to remember who had given you what and when. But the best part of playing 'Father Christmas' on this small scale was creeping around in the dark, stubbing our toes on those iron bedsteads and laughing all the way.

On Christmas mornings, when the Savage-Baileys were in charge, we had a special breakfast of boiled eggs, toast, jam and cereal. Then we put on our Sunday clothes and marched off, two by two, to church. Christmas dinner was always the best meal of the year: roast chicken, stuffing, roast potatoes and vegetables followed by plum pudding into which a few silver sixpenny bits had been buried. One remembered Christmas, Mr. Savage-Bailey's sister and brother-in-law, the actors Dulcie Gray and Michael Denison, came and had dinner with us. They were very nice and gave each of us five bob.

After dinner we listened to, and fidgeted through, the King's Speech, and then trooped down to the front hall for the tree. The Yule log was blazing and Father Christmas came down the stairs to the tree, which was all lit up with real candles. (It was most definitely a fire hazard, but we didn't know about things like that and I still remember how beautiful it looked). We received our postal money orders, one from the Committee and one from Mr. Coward, and then Father Christmas called out our names, – he sounded uncannily like Mr. Savage-Bailey – and we went up to get our presents. Some of us had been sent packages from relatives – Susannah and I were among those lucky ones. Some children were never sent anything from home, but kind staff members made sure they had something to open.

On Boxing Day, after we had written our 'Thank You' letters, those of us that had a place to go went there for the holidays.

There were lots of comings and goings during the Savage-Baileys' time. Matey Irvine left after her accident with the sewing machine and was replaced briefly by a Mrs. Collier. Then we had Mrs. Smith, who I dimly remember had a small son. A new group of children came to join us war babies: Liz, Caroline, Michael, Kenny, Carl, David, Sue and I. We had all been born during the Second World War, arriving at Silverlands as very small children shortly after it re-opened. Older than we were: Christopher, Ed, Brian, Leslie, Gerry, Madge, Valerie, Desmond, Paddy and Terry Mac had all arrived during the Aggitters' years, too.

With the Savage-Baileys came new children: Pauline, Triggy and Ann, all around Sue's age, joined the girls' wing and little Norma was put in care of Matron, being only four, as I had once been. Three brothers came but didn't stay long. Dave, Gerry, Charlie, Raymond, Paul and Nick moved in with the boys. Mrs. Hazell fostered Pauline's brother, Stephen and Dave's brother, Jonny, both only three when they came, for a year or two. Many of the older kids, who had reached the age of fifteen having learned all that Stepgates School had to offer, left Silverlands for London.

A promotional pamphlet called *The Story of Silverlands*, written for fund-raising and promotional purposes, noted the following development at this time:

> In 1949, the Committee realized a long-cherished ambition and bought No. 27 Rutland Gate, Kensington, for use as a hostel for children of training age; this happy and comfortable home is a great boon and solves the 'where to live while training' problem (which was a constant worry in the past) as well as providing the Fund's office accommodation.
>
> There is no set leaving age, as this depends on the profession or calling which the child adopts and the amount of training required before he or she can earn their own living, but they are usually able to do this by the time they are seventeen or eighteen years of age. Very few of the children become actors or actresses, although an outstanding exception is Mr. Frank Lawton.'

Number 27 Rutland Gate while it was part of the Actors' Orphanage, was run by Mr. and Mrs. Duncan Rider. Duncan Rider had himself been at both Langley Hall and Silverlands as a boy before the evacuation to America. He, being one of the older boys, did not go but enlisted instead. Yolande Rider, who became my sister's surrogate mother for a while, was an elegant and pretty French woman who Duncan had met during the war. They had a small son known to us all as 'Dunky.'

In spite of what that pamphlet said about very few children entering the theatre as a profession – and we were actively discouraged unless we showed talent – quite a few of us did enter the world of our parents.

As well as Ken, a.k.a. Peter who became a film director, Paddy went into stage management and his brother Terry Mac was a front-of-house manager at both the Old Vic and the National Theatre; Desmond acted many a role on the boards; Louis became a rock musician in South Africa and Canada; Tony went on to become a highly respected stage and television actor; and Ed, encouraged to join the Merchant Navy, left his ship, went to Canada and became a television producer. As our mother had hoped, my sister went into the theatre for a short time and eventually I, too, had a career in the arts, both in administration and as an actress and stage manager.

Once Rutland Gate was established, the older children moved in to begin their job training. Rozanne, Mina, Tony, Jimmy, Rodney, Carol and others left Silverlands for London that first year. Wendy, Ken, Madge, Paddy and my sister, Susannah, followed a year later, with Valerie, Peter, Leslie, Gerry, Terry Mac and Pauline all staying there before it closed in 1954.

My sister was precocious and charming, with curly hair and long legs. Our mother was convinced she had theatrical promise and wanted Susannah to go to acting school. Despite Noël Coward's admonitions to 'Mrs. Worthington', our mother was determined to put a daughter on the stage.

Mother had tried to put me on the stage, before we went to Silverlands, when I was a chubby and adorable three year old with a very 'ginny' voice; before my blonde curls turned mousey-brown and straight. Through her numerous contacts, she had arranged for me to meet a lady film producer and hoped that I would become 'England's answer to Shirley Temple!' I was scrubbed, put into my best green Liberty-print smocked dress with matching knickers, white socks and black patent leather shoes, and taken to the Savoy Hotel. There I was fed strawberries and cream, chocolate biscuits and other delicacies! While the rest of England was on rationing! Mother urged me to sing my party piece, which I usually sang out in broad Cockney:

O me taters and me 'ot fried fish, / You can eat 'em anyway you wish.
You can eat 'em on a plate or a dish, / Or on a little bit of paper!

Or, at least would I please say something! But I didn't. The only time I opened my mouth was to put food in it. Mother was very cross and never again did she try to put me on the stage. *Perhaps* that's *why she left me at Silverlands for all those years?*

Susannah had been something of a mischief-maker, always getting into trouble at Silverlands and causing problems for the staff. So, to appease the staff *and* Mother, the Committee agreed that Susannah, although only eleven, could live at Rutland Gate and attend the Arts Educational School. Formerly known as the Cone Ripman School, the Arts Educational School in Chiswick was, and still is, an independent secondary school that trains students from eleven to eighteen years to become dancers, actors and singers.

While she was there, Sue learned to dance and act and, showing promise, auditioned for and got several paying jobs. She was an Ovaltine-y on the radio and, with comedian Max Bygraves, she sang, *"I'm a pink toothbrush, you're a blue toothbrush,/Have we met somewhere before?/I'm a pink toothbrush and I think toothbrush/That we met at the bathroom door."* She toured with Margaret Lockwood and Felix Aylmer in Agatha Christie's *The Spider's Web*, and appeared in repertory theatres in a couple of plays at Salisbury and Frinton-on-Sea. Enrolled at the Cone Ripman, Sue lived at Rutland Gate until 1954, coming down to Silverlands, as most former 'orphans' did occasionally, on a weekend.

I was a shy and awkward child. If my sister was quicksilver, I was pudding dough. I was solid, almost inanimate in my shyness and usually had my nose buried in a book. Books were my escape: books and daydreaming. I read lots of books, especially books about children with families: Enid Blyton's *Famous Five* and *Adventure* series, Arthur Ransome's *Swallows and Amazons*; Mazo de la Roche's *Jalna* books – each of them several times, before moving on to the Brontes, Jane Austen and Dickens. I read and daydreamed whenever I could escape my taskmasters. I'd climb up into a favorite tree with a book and dream that I wasn't chubby, bespectacled little Judy Moore, but one of my current heroines.

After that first feeling of being left behind, I didn't really miss my sister very much. She had always been one of the older girls and they were often very bossy and quite mean to us little ones. I don't think Sue looked out for me because I was her sister. In my memory, I was just another little kid to be bossed around, but I do remember that first enormous sense of loss when she left. When she visited on weekends nothing had changed, she was still bossy, but she did give me her teddy bear, the one Father had given her. Teddy became my friend and confidant well into my teenage years.

After our father had left home, some well-meaning adult told us that the reason our parents had separated was that during the war Father was cashiered (or ritually dismissed) because he had embezzled £9 to buy Susannah a teddy bear for her birthday. For years, I thought it rather romantic, moving and sad that someone could be cashiered, all because he needed the money to buy his little daughter a present. It was true, he did buy Susannah that teddy bear for her third birthday, but Teddy was *not* why Father was cashiered.

I still have the bear, battered and torn, a reminder of my childhood and of the father I never knew. My sister's leaving for Rutland Gate was just another abandonment in a long line of them, and there were more to come. I read somewhere that *'the desolation of abandonment makes insecurity especially potent in children brought up by those who are not their parents.'* I was one such child. We were all such children.

The Savage-Baileys, who were much less savage than some of our other early warders, did try to make life special for us every now and then. They devised complicated Easter egg hunts all around the house and, on birthdays, each child was allowed to choose what they would like for pudding. My birthday, January 3rd, always fell when I was at my grandparents' or with Mother at some repertory theatre, so I never did get to choose my pudding. The Savage-Baileys were kind people and now, in hindsight, some of us remember them fondly; especially in light of what was to come.

I wish we had shown the Savage-Baileys more gratitude for their kindness and concern, but I am afraid we were a very unruly bunch of kids and took advantage of them and their good nature. Here's Noël Coward again:

Friday, 14 April 1950. Long Orphanage meeting. Children behaving very badly, insulting everyone and stealing left and right. Went over their menus and school reports. Interviewed Mr. Savage-Bailey, who stubbornly believes that sweet reason, kindliness and long moral explanations is the right way to handle a lot of illiterate young hooligans of very mixed parentage. It is becoming distressingly clear that his theory is not practicable. He is a kind little man, but like so many idealists, he is a cracking fool. The dear children obviously share my opinion and run rings around him.

And so, early in the following year, exit Mr. and Mrs. Savage-Bailey and enter Miss Berry followed a few months later by David Victor Gordon. None of our lives would ever be the same again.

SEVEN

Tales Out of School

1950 AND 1951 had brought many changes. The younger children left Lyne Primary School and the lower forms at Stepgates in Chertsey and went to Frithwald. My sister, at eleven, had left for Rutland Gate to join the other much older teenagers and to be spoiled by Mrs. Rider for the next four years. Sue left behind her at Silverlands her teddy bear, her little sister, and a lot of memories. She had achieved a rather intimidating reputation in the girls' wing. Ann, who arrived aged twelve at the beginning of 1950, remembers being offered the option of going into a dormitory with the big girls, Carol, Pamela and Valerie, all of whom were between 14 and 16, or rooming with the younger ones. Ann being shy opted for the younger girls and immediately became one of Sue's 'subjects,' even though Sue was younger than she. Liz, Triggy and, arriving soon after Ann, Pauline, were all under Sue's thumb until she left for Rutland Gate. Ann contracted German measles shortly after she arrived. Desperate to get them so she wouldn't have to go to school, Sue spent ages hanging on to Ann and ordering her to breathe on her. It didn't work – she never did get German measles.

Under the Savage-Baileys, the housemaster was Mr. Whitehouse who left rather suddenly, someone said it was for inappropriate behaviour, although we could only guess why he left and, of course, rumours flew. *Inappropriate* to our little minds meant S E X, but we never knew for sure. Mr. Weedon arrived to replace him and quickly became very popular. He had been a member of the British Olympic team and he always wore a jacket showing off his badges. He taught us all kinds of athletic skills, at most of which I failed miserably. Mr. Weedon and the boys played cricket and football and we all had gymnastics. He also taught us how to swing Indian clubs, which was brave of him.

It was while Mr. Savage-Bailey was headmaster that we started dancing classes on Monday evenings in the Assembly room. The classes continued for a couple of years and stopped during Miss Berry's reign. The girls wore little green cotton tunics that had splits up the sides and green bloomers to match. Some of the boys took the class, too, but they just wore shorts and white shirts, no bloomers for them.

"Christopher was very good at those jump things." Ann wrote, "I can't remember the name of them. You took a sort of leap across the floor and turned at the same time. Carl was a good dancer too, but then he was good at everything athletic, and so was Janet."

When members of the Committee came down, we would put on a little show for them. The kids who were really good, like my sister or Janet, did solo pieces every time. Then we all would do a little dance, in a sort of chorus line, to a simple song. One number was *I'm a Little Teapot Short and Stout*, but I always tipped too late. After Sue had left, once and only once, I was given a solo and I did a little song and dance to *Me and My Teddy Bear* – my mother's daughter for one brief shining moment.

I lived in awe of my big sister during those early years. Even though Sue was bossy, she was popular because she was always full of fun and mischief. While Ann was the eldest in their dormitory, Sue was often put in charge by the staff because she had the ability to rule the others with a rod of iron.

When we four first arrived in early 1947, Sue and Liz went to Lyne Primary School and Caroline and I stayed at Silverlands until we were five. The next year Sue was old enough to go to Stepgates School in Chertsey with the older children, while Caroline and I joined Liz and some of the boys at Lyne. Peter, Valerie, Sue and Brian all remember Stepgates with loathing. In the 1940s and '50s, Stepgates was a County school offering general education. Basically, in those days, it was a holding place until students reached fifteen, the legal school leaving age.

Every morning, the older kids walked down the driveway to the bottom of Holloway Hill and waited for the green double decker bus on the Guildford Road. By the bus stop was a ditch that in the spring, or after a heavy rain, became more of a stream. Waiting for the bus they often played *Tarzan*, swinging across on a branch, often falling in and going to school with wet feet or worse, wet bums. Sue was swinging across the ditch one day and got her groin caught on some barbed wire. When she arrived sore and bleeding at Stepgates, she was told to lift her skirt while the teacher painted *New Skin* on her wound in front of the whole class. Stepgates' days were numbered after a male teacher molested Valerie and she reported him.

Throughout those early school days, advantage was taken of us both by teachers and other students, probably because of our parentless state. We all attended the two local day schools in sizable groups and, consequently, it was 'us against them' during lunch break. We had more fights than not with the townies. Sometimes, seemingly against the odds, we made friends with the local kids and some of us even became attracted to those of the opposite sex. Madge was grounded for weeks when she climbed down the ivy outside her bedroom to meet a reform school boy she knew from Stepgates.

When I turned five, and for the next two years, we younger ones walked down the back drive past the piggery and along Lyne Lane to school. Lyne Primary was a stone building on the other side of the long hedge bordering Trinity Church graveyard. There were two small cloakrooms, one on each end of the building, and one large classroom with a folding partition down the middle for when our teacher Miss B. had an assistant once a week and we could be divided into more manageable groups.

Miss B. ruled the school with a ruler. Any disobedience or inattention was met with a whack across the knuckles, or worse the back of the knees, with her wooden ruler which seemed to be an extension of her right hand. If you were persistently naughty, you had to stand in the corner and wear a dunce's cap. I was always being punished for daydreaming and not paying attention until I was six. That was when the visiting school nurse had me read an eye chart and it was discovered that I wasn't daydreaming, I simply couldn't see the blackboard or the teacher. Everything and everyone was a blur. I was issued some bottle-bottomed thick, round, wire-framed National Health glasses and suddenly things came into focus – and the nasty nicknames started: Owly! Four Eyes! Judibugs! This last one, which started out meaning bug-eyed, eventually became a friendly nickname. Liz still calls me that sometimes.

At Lyne, if you needed to go to the lavatory you had to raise your hand and say, 'Please Miss, may I be excused?' (For years, I thought that was a euphemism for going to the loo). If she gave permission, you went outside the building and across the playground to a long wooden hut, partially open to the elements, with an entrance for girls on one end and boys on the other. There were three holes on each side with only a wooden plywood board separating the boys from the girls. In winter, those wooden seats were icy cold and all the time they were invariably wet. In summer, the stench was awful. You could look down into the hole and see what had gone before. I'm sure they were only cleaned out once a week – if then. Sitting on a wooden, splintery disc, with your legs dangling and your knickers round your ankles, a beastly boy could climb up and look at you over the top of the wall. There wasn't much you could do in that position – except, get even later.

Lyne Primary marked the beginning of my formal education and the only thing I remember about it, educationally speaking, was the large map of the world that Miss B. would pull down for our geography lesson. With her ruler she would tap some small piece of pink on the map and ask, "Now children, who can tell me which part of the British Empire this is?" I can still remember where Bechuanaland, Rhodesia and Ceylon were – only they aren't called that now and they aren't pink anymore.

In 1950, we left Lyne Primary and Stepgates, where education had been rudimentary at best, and were enrolled in better schools. The older kids, those who hadn't yet left for Rutland Gate, went to the new secondary modern schools, Fullbrook and Halliford. A very few finished up their schooling at Stepgates. Brian was one of those. He said, "I had a poor record for schoolwork." Unlike those going up to London to prepare for the work-world, Brian stayed on for a few years after leaving school as Bert Hazell's assistant.

About twenty of us, between six and thirteen, were sent to Frithwald House School. We had started at Frithwald during the time of the Savage-Baileys who, being concerned for our welfare, had recommended that we all attend better schools. We were at Frithwald all through the rocky years with Miss Berry and Mr. Gordon and we left when Mr. Fraser left. It was at Frithwald that the world of books, music and languages came into our lives, and it was at Frithwald where I began to receive the education for which I have been grateful ever since.

Frithwald House School was a private school, off Pyrcroft Road in Chertsey, for boys and girls up to thirteen years. Mrs. Sheelagh Grimsley, who lived in the main house with her two daughters, ran the school. Anna Grimsley was Susannah's age and she was so very fair, with pale skin and white-blond hair, that she looked almost albino. Sue and Anna quickly became best friends, much to Ann's dismay because she had thought Sue was *her* special friend. But Sue left them both, after only one term, for Rutland Gate, acting school and the bright lights of London.

At Frithwald, after the first few weeks in our shabby, second-hand clothes, we were issued with uniforms, grey wool trimmed with maroon. The girls wore grey skirts and white blouses in the winter and felt hats that quickly shrunk in the first rain and looked like silly bumps on our heads. In the summer, we had maroon and white checked frocks and straw panama hats. The boys wore long shorts on their short legs, white shirts and maroon ties. We all wore grey blazers and grey knee socks that fell, concertina-like, around our ankles before we were even halfway to school prompting Mrs. Grimsley to say every day in greeting: "Pull up your socks, children."

In good weather we all walked to Frithwald from Silverlands in a crocodile. (*Why was it called a crocodile? Why not a snake or a centipede?*) Anyway, we walked two by two to the beginning of Chertsey town and over the railway bridge where a teacher would meet us and walk us the rest of the way. When it rained, and it often did, we took the bus to Chertsey Station and walked from there. Lots of wet mackintoshes and muddy shoes were hung about the small cloakroom.

On the way to school, along Pycroft Road, was a cluster of council houses. One day, not long after we had started going to Frithwald, Charlie noticed a strange square white light in one of the front rooms. Soon, all twenty of us were standing on the lawn, gawping in the window at this wooden box with little black and white people moving around inside it. Television had come to Chertsey!

Frithwald had rather a rudimentary set up for a school. In the main house, which was old with low ceilings, the youngest children had lessons. All the Silverlands children were served a hot midday meal in the house, cooked for us by an elderly deaf, or was she retarded?, woman. Only the two Grimsley daughters ate those hot meals with us, the other pupils brought sandwiches and ate them in their classrooms. The red-headed twins, Janet and Dorothy, always brought marmalade sandwiches for lunch. That's how Liz and I always remember them; marmalade sandwiches, big teeth and curly red hair.

Another Frithwald student was Leonie. The daughter of a wealthy Scottish laird, Leonie lived in a little cottage on the Guildford Road with an elderly couple who were paid to take care of her. Leonie was in my class. While her real age was sixteen, and she was tall with a well-developed bust, she was emotionally and mentally about seven. A big amiable girl, with long brown plaits and a Scottish burr, she would do anything asked of her. When one of the boys said, "Leonie, drink your ink." She tipped the ink from her inkwell down her throat and, with her mouth gaping and dark blue, she roared with laughter along with all of us, until the teacher came in and admonished us for being cruel.

While Mrs. Grimsley taught the younger children in her house, the others were taught in two classrooms in a rough sort of Quonset hut in a back corner of the property. Cow pastures on two sides added to the rustic feeling. Both classrooms were heated by one central coal stove. With only three classrooms in all, several ages learned together. We learned arithmetic, geography, history, English grammar, Latin and French. During lunch, we had to speak French or not speak at all. It was very quiet at lunchtime. Just the occasional *"Voulez vous passé le sal?"* and *"Merci beaucoup."*

There were two other teachers besides Mrs. Grimsley. One was young and attractive and I've forgotten her name. Michael developed a crush on her. On the way home from school he told us that it was really *she* who was in love with him and that *she* had tried to seduce *him*. We all laughed at him, "Fat chance, Michael!" But Michael was rather a romantic as a boy, – always a would-be Romeo. Later in life he was troubled and he died in his sixties after a long illness.

The other teacher, Mrs. Eyre, was older. She had a daughter who was my age with a husky voice and a wicked sense of humour. Mary Jane taught me how to cut a peashooter from a hollow stemmed plant. I don't know what the plant was but it looked like rhubarb and its stems were perfect for peashooters. She and I used to make our own and shoot peas and bits of paper at the boys, both during and out of class.

Mrs. Grimsley had long grey hair which she wore loose and, it seemed to me, she always greeted us wearing a long cloak over an equally long dress. When I read about witches – both good ones and wicked ones – I always imagine them looking rather like Mrs. Grimsley, although I know she was a kind woman with our welfare at heart.

I think her school was rather *alternative* as schools went in those days, leaning towards A. S. Neill's *Summerhill* philosophy. A games master came once a week and made us do calisthenics in the big playing field just beyond a nasty little swimming pool. We Silverlanders had to clean out that pool each year, probably as a way of reducing our school fees, which must have been sizeable. We cleaned that dirty, slimy pool as best we could every May until the year of the big polio scare. Then the pool became off-limits to everyone and we were all vaccinated against polio.

It was in February 1952 and we were all in class – by then I had moved up from Form 1A in the house to Form Upper 1A in the Quonset hut – when Mrs. Grimsley came in holding some lengths of wide black ribbon and looking sad.

She said in a low, hushed voice, "Our good King is dead, children." And she gave each of us a piece of ribbon and a safety pin. "Class is suspended for the day." she said, "Now I want you to help each other pin a black armband on your left blazer sleeve. When you have done so, I want you all to quietly think about the dear King and about his young daughter, who will have a very difficult job ahead of her as our Queen."

We did as we were told and, with long faces and crocodile tears, we acted being sad because it was expected of us. Later, we all crowded into Mrs. Grimsley's sitting room and saw the dowager Queen Mary, the widowed Queen and the young princesses on a very small television set. They all looked very tiny and stiff.

Noël Coward bought us a big television set the following year, in time to see the coronation of our new Queen, Elizabeth II.

At Frithwald the teachers didn't pick on us, in fact Mrs. Grimsley, according to the old Committee minutes, was concerned, and somewhat critical of our minders, in her early reports. When we first went there, she had commented on our shabby clothing – that's probably when and why we got school uniforms. She also complained that there was no supervision of our homework, and there was a lack of cooperation between her teachers and the Silverlands staff about each individual child.

> *I never remember ever having any help or supervision with my homework, not even later when life got better. I had to slog through it by myself, but the homework we got at Frithwald was fairly simple. It was later at Perkins that, alone, I had to find my way each evening through the forests of Latin and French pluperfects, dangling participles and compound adjectives, theorems and trigonometry, and, oh horrors, physics.*

Mrs. Grimsley also expressed concern that no one from the Committee turned out for Parents' Days. *Well, neither did any of our parents!* On Parents' Day, we all performed short plays, sang songs and played simple *etudes* for all the *other* children's parents. An old upright piano was rolled outside onto the newly mowed front lawn for the occasion and folding chairs were set up for visiting grown-ups. Each and everyone of Frithwald's student body had to participate. We either leapt from the bushes in some form of bizarre dance, or sang some old English folk song: *Sweet Lass of Richmond Hill* (the boys) or *Soldier, Soldier will you marry me with your musket, fife and drum* (the girls). At the close of each Parents' Day was prize giving. I still have my four little red leather bound classics: Form prize three years in a row and once, but never ever again, a prize for arithmetic.

While I was at Frithwald, and Susannah was in London learning to sing, dance and act, our mother suddenly took an interest in me, *perhaps because I had won prizes?* Anyway, whatever the reason, I quote the minutes of an Actors' Orphanage Committee meeting on 29 November 1952:

In view of her (Judy's) very favourable prospects, the Committee approved Miss Joan White's action in entering her daughter for St.Helen's, Northwood, and endorsed her proposal also to cover the future by entering Judy for St. Paul's Girls School, Hammersmith at the same time.

Cover the future? Was Mother hedging her bets that *I* wouldn't get a scholarship to one school, so try the other? Well, *I* didn't want to go to either but *I was never asked!*

Mrs. Grimsley, who thought kindly of my potential, did enter me for St. Paul's and also for the Surrey County Council's 11-plus exam for the local grammar school in Chertsey. I didn't get into St Paul's or St Helen's, much to my relief, and I did pass the 11-plus and so, in 1954 I went from Frithwald to Sir William Perkins Grammar School for Girls, whose junior school, Pyrcroft, was just around the corner.

Silverlands children went to Frithwald from the autumn of 1950 until July of 1955. The older ones moved on to Halliford, Fulbrook, and several other Secondary Modern schools in the area, there were to be no more large groups of us at any one school. The littlest children went to Ottershaw Primary for a short time, where some remember having the teacher check their heads, every week, for lice. Later, the little ones went back to Lyne. Terry, arriving at Silverlands in late 1952, had taken and passed the 11-plus and joined Christopher at Woking Grammar School. Ann left Frithwald in 1952 to go to Guildford Day Commercial and take a secretarial course. With so many of us leaving Frithwald in 1954, the student body became seriously depleted but the school continued on until the early 1970s. It was a small and friendly school and we were treated with care there.

EIGHT

Tripe

THE SAVAGE-BAILEYS HAD left in 1951 and were replaced by the unlovely Miss Berry. She was a large grey woman with grey hair and glasses; actually she wasn't just large, she was fat and when she got cross her flesh shook like tapioca pudding (which incidentally alternated with Stodge as our 'afters'). I don't recall her ever actually hitting us but, in her own way, she was a mistress of sadism and creative chastisement. When Mr. Gordon arrived to replace Mr. Weedon as housemaster, the two of them were a match made in hell. She delegated all corporal punishment to him, and he clearly enjoyed it.

Perhaps it's because she was so fat that I associate her mainly with bad food stories. I remember her so vividly towering over the hot plate, swaying back and forth, watching every move we made with her little piggy eyes as we ate and gagged. She favoured mauve or grey solid colored dresses so that her affect was of a large, dull mound. She would stand behind that huge hot plate, laden with the big platters of grey meat and bowls of soggy vegetables, wielding a large serving spoon with which she plopped the food onto our plates.

A lot has been written about the old days of British *bas cuisine* and the role it played in its institutions, thus promoting England's reputation for serving truly disgusting food. Novels and films of schooldays in 'jolly old England,' for example *Tom Brown's School Days*, *The Belles of Saint Trinian's* and *Oliver Twist*, all featured bad food as a central part of child rearing. Thankfully those days are mostly history.

When I was small, the food at Silverlands exemplified all the worst jokes about British cooking. Granted it was after the war, with rationing still on, and cooking for fifty plus children and staff, day in and day out, was probably a strain on any cook's creativity. But those early cooks'

85

styles never varied: boil all vegetables until they are mush and cook all meat to a uniform grey, *perhaps to disguise its age and origin.*

The predictability of those early meals has also stayed with me. Breakfast was *always* lumpy porridge in the winter, dry cereal in the summer, followed by a slab of squishy white bread anointed with a smear of margarine and a drop of watery jam — for several years war-surplus tins of peach and melon jam. This jam had an odour so strong and redolent you could smell it all the way down the driveway. Brian suggested the reason we could smell it along the drive was because some enterprising kid had buried some of it to finally be rid of it. Some of the older kids even took up a collection — tuppence a person — to go and buy some other kind of jam; anything as long as it wasn't peach and melon.

Lunch, except on weekends, was served at our various day schools and was no culinary delight there either: Spam sandwiches at Lyne and hot meals of indeterminate stews and soups at both Frithwald and Perkins. When we returned from school, we had high tea at five o'clock and at that meal, in case you forgot what day it was, the menu was there to remind you: Monday, baked beans on toast; Tuesday, scrambled (powdered) eggs on toast; Wednesday, sardines on toast; Thursday, macaroni with cheese-substitute and, inevitably, boiled fish every Friday — week in and week out. For three years we had dried haddock every week, the cooks boiled it so much that when served up it looked like a washed-out piece of old rag. All vegetables were mashed: swedes, turnips, marrow (zeppelin-sized courgettes), watery spinach, overcooked cabbage, and potatoes. *Bubble and Squeak* was served on Fridays with the haddock. This gourmet dish of leftover cabbage and potatoes cooked in lard is still considered an English delicacy and, like *Toad in the Hole*, when cooked with care and seasoning it can be quite tasty. Rarely did we eat anything that was seasoned, in the late forties or early fifties, except sometimes with too much salt.

On weekends, the fare was similar except on Christmas Day and Easter Sunday when, with the coming of the Savage-Baileys, we had roast chicken and roasted potatoes and that tradition, happily, continued thereafter.

Pudding was 'Stodge' in several disguises or slimy tapioca pudding looking like frog spawn. 'Stodge' is better known as Suet Pudding. Sometimes, this was served in a square shape and smeared, sparingly, with jam unless it was blackberry season and we had picked enough (and not eaten too many) from the prolific bushes at the edge of the woods. Sometimes the 'Stodge' came disguised in a long, cylindrical shape and studded with raisins, a delicacy still known as *Spotted Dick*. We used to think the etymology behind its name had something to do with its shape, but it was probably named after some ancient serf. 'Stodge' was usually served with a white substance resembling Brylcreem and with the consistency of library paste. A mealtime game was to get the Brylcreem between the 'Stodge' and your plate, hold the plate upside down and see how long it took for it to fall off. Sometimes it never did.

Meal times began with the banging of the gong, following the ringing of the tower bell summoning us indoors to wash our hands. At the sound of the gong, we queued up outside the dining room. After hands were inspected and pronounced clean enough, we filed inside to pick up a thick white china plate and queued up again in front of the hot plate. There, the staff member on duty, often the head, would lob a dollop of the day's delicacy onto our plate. (The staff ate later than we did in the early days. They probably couldn't stand our noise or the sound of gagging *and* I'm sure they got better food.)

Then, we took our regular places at one of the long green Formica tables and stood behind our chairs until everyone had been served. *If you were good and arrived early, you got to eat your food cold.* Once we were all served, the staff member in charge said, "Charlie (or whoever), please say grace" and Charlie would say, without taking a breath, *'for-what-we-are-about-to-receive-may-the-Lord-make-us-truly-thankful-amen'* and, with much scraping of chairs, we sat down and tucked in.

Every meal was washed down with a cup of tea, – no juice or milk for us, and fizzy drinks were almost unheard of then. The tea was made in the pantry across the hall. The girls, naturally in those days, always made the tea and set the tables.

Here's how to make Silverlands tea: first dump a pound of loose tea leaves into an enormous metal tea pot (big enough for four dozen dormice), next add sugar, a quart of milk and fill with boiling water; pour, with the help of another person and without the aid of a strainer, into china mugs on a trolley and serve. I was staying at my grandmother's when I realised that milk and sugar were usually added separately, to one's personal taste. Personal taste was not something that was encouraged at Silverlands then.

At the end of each meal, after the closing grace was said (*'For-what-we-have-received-may-the-lord-make-us-truly-thankful-amen'*), a booming voice announced,

'Carl and Ann, washing up.'

Liz was on washing up with Gerry one day. "There was some red Jell-o left in a bowl," she said, "this Jell-o was from the staff's meal. WE didn't get Jell-o."

A Jell-o fight ensued. Liz doesn't remember who lobbed the first glob, but she remembers red Jell-o spattered all over the pantry. Matron caught them and made them clean it up.

We had to eat everything on our plates. If we didn't or couldn't finish, we got it cold and congealed for breakfast. Sometimes, the food was so inedible we gagged. Caroline once threw up onto her plate. Miss Berry stood over her and made her eat her own sick.

It was during Miss Berry's tour of duty that we were served tripe for the first (and last) time. Now this was not your gourmet *Tripe a la mode de Caen*, it was plain boiled tripe. If you don't know what tripe is, let me just tell you it is the lining of a cow's stomach. It's offal and it is truly awful. It was served for one Sunday's lunch.

Returning from church, we noticed that the entire house stunk of something vile. Silverlands was a very big house and this smell permeated the whole building. It smelled as though something very big had died, as indeed it had. The gong rang. We lined up, as usual, picked up our plates and were served a disgusting pale, gelatinous mess, colour-coordinated with loathsome mashed turnips and lumpy mashed potatoes. The source of the smell that had stunk up the house was on our plates.

We slunk to our places. Grace was said and, reluctantly, we sat down to eat the white mounds in front of us. I picked at the tripe and put a little in my mouth. I gagged. It tasted even worse than it smelled. I looked around. Almost everyone was having the same reaction but, at my table, Terry Mac was eating the stuff and actually enjoying it. There were always about eight or ten of us at each table, with big and little boys and girls at each.

I was a few years younger than Terry Mac and yet he was always fun to horse around with. He had come to Silverlands a few months after Sue and I with his older brother Paddy. He had an unruly shock of hair that seemed to stand straight up on his head no matter how long it grew, lots of pimples and a sweet disposition. He, like so many of us, survived our childhood by having a sense of humour, and his was one of the craziest. He was always clowning around (he could contort his face into very strange shapes) like getting up on an upside-down rubbish basket to conduct an imaginary symphony or riding backwards on a bike. And now he was actually *eating* the tripe and he seemed to be enjoying it! As soon as those seated next to him realised this, they began to give him theirs and just ate their vegetables.

I was too far down the table to slide mine onto his plate and anyway, he said he'd had enough. What to do? The stuff made me gag and I didn't want to throw up and be made to eat regurgitated tripe. Nor did I want it cold for breakfast. Then, I had a brainwave. In those days, we girls wore navy blue knickers and these thick cotton knickers had a little pocket on the left front side. I had never known what that little pocket was for before, but I did now. It was there to put tripe in! Surreptitiously, I picked up my slimy portion in my left hand and oozed it into my knickers' pocket. Then, as nonchalantly as possible, I ate my potatoes and turnips.

After we were dismissed, I quickly ran outside and fed my tripe to the dogs. They loved it, especially Miss Berry's big fat Golden Retriever. But that smell stayed with me for days. We had been issued with our weekly clean clothes as usual on Saturday evening and so my tripe-y knickers would have to last me all week.

Liz and Carl sat at a different table from me. Carl, who was from Scotland, always wore his kilt on Sundays. Being sweet on Liz at the time, he put his and Liz's tripe into his sporran. Now, isn't that what sporrans are for? In the end, since so many of us couldn't stomach the tripe, Miss Berry gave up and after the meal, the trolley, on which we piled our plates, had tripe and glutinous white gravy dripping over the edge. "It was a disgusting sight!" said Ann, who was on washing up that day.

I have never eaten tripe since, no matter how grand the restaurant or elegant the recipe.

Sometimes, staff members used food as a form of punishment. The Aggitters had the Defaulters Table, where transgressors sat and ate only bread and water having either been caught talking after lights-out or coming late to meals or chores or for any number of other crimes and misdemeanors. Considering the menu in those days, it wasn't such a bad punishment. Other food-related punishments were plucking freshly killed chickens or washing eggs (after Mr. Fraser introduced the chickens), or sitting out in the courtyard sentenced to peel potatoes by the hundreds. We ate a lot of potatoes.

We were growing kids and often hungry, so we generally ate our starchy food like good girls and boys. Our meals weren't always terrible, it depended on who was cooking, and they definitely improved as time went on. For a short time in 1955, two young women, graduates of a culinary school, came and the food was, all too briefly, delicious.

To supplement our diet, we relied on Mother Nature. The fields and the woods beyond were filled with nut trees and berry bushes. Our hunter-gatherer instincts prevailed most of the time and we managed to find food that was not poisonous and only occasionally gave us tummy aches and the trots. There were also the neighbors' apple orchards where we went scrumping and, in the late summer, on the edge of the woods the blackberries were plentiful. When we were sent out with big wooden pails to pick them for the cook, we ate almost as many as we brought back. There were wild plum and cherry trees whose fruits we ate before their time and got stomach cramps or ate after their time and gained added protein from the worms. And there were plenty of nut trees: beech nuts with three little triangular nuts in shiny brown shells which, in turn, were encased in hard spikey shells – a lot of work, but very tasty; hazelnut trees resulting in many cracked molars; and there were the bountiful chestnuts.

Eating chestnuts were as plentiful as horse chestnuts, and when they fell to the ground, bursting out of their spiny burrs, they provided many feasts for hungry kids. When Mr. Fraser came we had 'Chibby' nights. Come autumn, we would build bonfires and roasted chestnuts in the embers until they turned black and cracked, then we poked the nuts out of the fire with a stick, blew on them until they cooled a little, peeled off that crispy casing and ate the hot roasted chestnut inside. Singing songs around the fire, punctuated with cries of "ooh" and "aah" as hot chestnuts were tossed from hand to hand to cool before the shell and membrane could be removed and the nut meat popped, still piping hot, into our mouths, that was so much fun. The smell of roast chestnuts, each winter from New York City sidewalk vendors, would take me right home to Silverlands.

For several years, the highlight of our young lives was Saturday afternoon when, having finished our chores and received our pocket money, Mr. Lazell arrived. Mr. Lazell was the Sweetie man. He parked his black Austin in the inner courtyard, opened his boot (trunk) and revealed an Ali Baba's cave of delights. Clutching our three-penny and sixpenny bits, we clustered around, waiting our turn. He had Rowntrees Fruit Pastilles and Fruit Gums, Aero, Crunchies, Black Magic and Caramello bars, Smarties, sherbet straws, gobstoppers, aniseed balls, licorice laces and Licorice Allsorts. And he had fizzy drinks. Tizer. a sort of orange and lemon mix, Lemon and Orange Squash and Dandelion and Burdock, which, despite its funny name, was actually very tasty.

Oh, what heaven it was just to gaze into his boot! But then you had to choose. With less than a shilling, the choices were few. Susannah came down on weekends in those days. She would buy a Crunchie bar and, if it was summer, take it up onto the air-raid shelter roof and let it melt in its wrapper. Then she'd lick it off her fingers and give some to Peter – she had always had a crush on Peter. Liz liked those fizzy sherbet straws which you opened at one end and sucked up the fizzy powder; most of it went up your nose. Me, I liked gobstoppers best because they were big and lasted all day, *and* they changed colour as they got smaller. I could suck on one for a while and then take it out of my mouth and wrap it in a piece of Jeyes toilet paper. Then I'd put it in my pocket and save it for the next day. (Jeyes toilet paper, hard like wax paper, was the only toilet paper my bottom knew until I arrived in America.)

Mr. Lazell came every Saturday. Nick, who came several years after me and was five years younger, remembers Mr. Lazell with equal fondness. Nick wrote from New Zealand,

> I remember Mr. Lazell coming every Saturday morning in his little Austin from his sweet shop in Ottershaw to bring us sherbet dabs and Tizer. I had just bought my Tizer in its glass bottle one Saturday morning and promptly dropped it on the concrete courtyard where it smashed. I shed lots of tears. I only got seven pence pocket money each week then. Mr. Lazell also sold those small lead cap bombs held together with string – you put a cap in the middle and dropped it and 'Bang'.

Before the advent of Mr. Lazell, there were sweet jars in the hall cupboard and we were allowed one or two small sweets on Sundays – if we'd been good. But Mr. Lazell, who arrived in the courtyard with the new decade, was the highlight of our young lives. To have your pocket money stopped was a fate worse than tripe

NINE

Playing with Fire

ALL THROUGH OUR childhood the years seemed to be defined by who was headmaster, or headmistress in Miss Berry's case, but there were other staff members who came and went, too: cooks, a laundress, housemasters and mistresses and a matron to attend to our physical and medical needs.

After Matey Irvine left early in 1950, we had a succession of matrons; none of them seem to have lasted more than six months. Maybe we were horrible children. Maybe the pay was bad. Maybe they were not very good at their jobs. Possibly all of the above. Whatever the reason, they came and they went and they left little or no impression on my young mind. I don't even remember most of their names.

There was one who we all seem to remember by her nickname, the Moon Lady. She would stand at her window, gazing out at the moon and sing to it – well, sort of moan really. Outside the matron's rooms, which were at the end of the hall in the girls' wing, was the flat roof of the library. Some of the bolder girls would climb out and spy on her. One night we could all hear her chanting so Liz, Triggy and Pauline crept down the hall after lights-out and huddled outside her door to listen. Suddenly, the door was flung open and a pot of cold tea was dumped on their heads. She left soon after that.

The next matron to arrive was Mrs.'Wiggy'Williams. There was a to-do with her that I remember well; somebody took her wig out of her room during the night. Of course, we all knew she wore a wig, though we never saw her without it. Kenny told us he had been standing behind her one time and saw the label sticking out the back. Even to *our* uninformed eyes it wasn't a very good wig. It was an unnatural red with tight curls resembling doll's hair. A couple of times her part was definitely in the wrong place when she came sailing into our dormitory in the early morning, stripping the sheets and thin blankets off our night-shirted bodies and singing out, "Rise and shine, ladies of the *corps de ballet*." We never asked why she woke us like that, or even what a *corps de ballet* was. Perhaps she was trying to be funny, but at six o'clock on a cold winter morning, being rapidly exposed to the frigid dormitory air, it was not very funny. The boys never had much to do with the matrons; they only went to them to get a sticking plaster on a cut, a teaspoon of castor oil for constipation or when, rarely, they were confined to the sanitarium. We girls had a parade of matrons looking over us all the time because Matron's room was on our corridor.

Anyway, one morning 'Wiggy' didn't appear and Doris the assistant cook-cum-laundress came and woke us instead.

"Where's Mrs. Williams?" we asked, secretly hoping she had died or left during the night. "She's indisposed." said Doris, "Now get up, you lot, and get down to breakfast before the gong goes or you wont get none."

Doris could be quite mean and we knew she reported us to Matron or Miss Berry frequently. I don't think she liked us very much. I know I didn't like her because she reported me for swinging on the clothesline and I was punished for it. Ann said she thought Doris was quite nice, but then Doris probably never caught her doing anything forbidden.

That morning, we all trooped down to breakfast and lined up for our lumpy porridge and slab of white bread with the yellowish lard that was supposed to resemble butter but was really lard with a yellow color capsule that girls on kitchen duty had to knead into the lard to make it look like butter – but it didn't ever look like butter, it was all streaky and it certainly didn't taste like the butter I had at my Gran's. We stood behind our chairs at the long green Formica topped tables. Someone said grace and we were just about to sit down when Miss Berry banged on the hot plate with a spoon and announced,

"Children, there will not be any breakfast until the individual who took a ...er...very personal item from Mrs. Williams' room last night comes forward and returns it to me. (Pause) Now, will the culprit come forward?'

Nobody moved, so Miss Berry said,

"Then, you shall *all* be punished. There will be no breakfast for anyone this morning, and instead of eating you will now get up and search this house and the grounds, too, until you find Mrs. Williams' missing … er…hairpiece. And you will forgo your pocket money this week and have double chores on Saturday, unless it is found. Dismiss."

We all shuffled out.

Janet said, "It has to be one of the big boys. They are the only ones who would do something like that. Come on, let's look in the front hall."

Liz, Janet and I went into the front hall and half-heartedly looked around the stairs and up the chimney. Then Janet went into the foyer.

"Come here, quick!" she whispered.

She was giggling. Liz and I went there and we immediately saw why. There, sitting jauntily on top of the bronze bust of Sir Gerald du Maurier, distinguished actor and past President of the Actors Orphanage Fund, was one red wig.

"Sssh," said Liz, "we mustn't say we found it or they'll think we took it. Lets just go to school."

So we did. We went to the back door and got our coats from the cloakroom and headed outside to catch the bus for Frithwald.

That evening at supper we noticed that Terry Mac and Charlie were missing. Miss Berry announced that the wig thieves had been caught and were being punished. How the boys were found out, we never did know but some of us suspected a tattletale had overheard them plotting and told Miss Berry, just to get in her good graces.

'Wiggy' Williams didn't stay long after that. She wasn't a bad old stick, but I think once she knew that we knew about her wig, it was hard to face us. She was last of our short-term matrons. Miss Rennie, who stayed for more than four years, arrived while Gordon was there, and she may well have helped to get rid of him.

Miss Berry probably found it difficult handling a rowdy bunch of children such as we were, especially the boys, and while I was at Silverlands, there were always many more boys than girls. Mr. Weedon stayed for only a few months as housemaster under Miss Berry. When he left, Mr.

Gordon came and, by the time he left, all of us were damaged physically and emotionally – some very severely.

Mr. Gordon arrived in 1952 and even now I shudder as I think of him. What he did to us has affected me in so many ways: fear of authority, years of feeling subordinate to most men and, a deep-seated fear of fire.

Bernie told me in 1981, when I had lunch with him in London, that one time, twenty years after he had left Silverlands, he had seen Gordon across the street in Guildford. Bernie said he had had to resist an overpowering urge to cross over and punch him.

For the majority of the children, who lived at Silverlands during that time, it took less than a year for Mr. Gordon to single-handedly impair our childhood memories. The Aggitters' caning and other punishments were nothing next to his. He was a sadistic brute.

David Victor Gordon was bull-necked and broad-shouldered with squinty eyes that were close together, a broken nose and gingery close-cropped hair. Although he wasn't very tall, he was very strong – a fitness fanatic and a bully.

Brian, who was almost fifteen when Gordon came, remembered Gordon particularly well. Gordon was primarily in charge of the boys and so he slept in the boys' wing. Shortly after he arrived, he called all the boys together and said to them,

"Which one of you is the best wrestler?"

They all pointed at Brian and said, "He is, sir." He pulled Brian forward, grabbed him by the neck and put a wrestling hold on him that made it impossible to move. He hurt Brian so badly that the pain brought tears to his eyes.

The boys had to do P.T. every day and if they didn't do it to his satisfaction, he would hit them. He also had them juggle Indian Clubs and do calisthenics, which Brian remembered actually enjoying. On Saturday afternoons after lunch, we had always gone down to the playing field for organised games or to watch the boys play cricket or football (soccer). When Gordon was housemaster, each time after games were over, he would yell at us, "Last one up to the house gets a hiding. So move it, you lot."

And so Liz and I, who were short and chubby, and those kids who were even smaller and younger than we were, would all run as fast as our little legs could go. Inevitably, it was always one of the little ones who got to the 'Rec' room last. Then Gordon would put that child over his knee and spank him or her. *Liz and I now think he probably got some kind of sick thrill from this.*

One Saturday after games, fourteen year-old Brian hung back on purpose. We all arrived in the recreation room, puffing and panting, Brian deliberately lagging behind us. Gordon was furious. He was probably looking forward to spanking a small girl or sickly boy. He grabbed a chair and threw it at Brian. Brian caught it and threw it back. Gordon then proceeded to beat Brian severely, while we all watched, numb with terror.

During my early years, we all went through spates of what used to be called bad habits but these are now seen as signs of some nervous disturbances. During Gordon's time bedwetting increased, as did thumb sucking and nail biting. I was a nail-biter, but not a bed-wetter; those children who wet the bed would have their noses rubbed in their urine-soaked sheets the next morning. Several children sucked their thumbs (my sister sucked two fingers on her right hand for years, even well past her time at Rutland Gate). Janet and I chewed our nails until we left Silverlands and, I'm told, I sometimes ground my teeth at night, too. If we were caught with our hands near our mouths we got our knuckles rapped or our fingers painted with Bitter Aloes. My fingers were painted so often that actually I grew to enjoy the taste. Caroline would get so nervous when she had to go to the bathroom, that she would dance up and down, legs locked together, outside the lavatory door unable to unlock her legs, until she almost wet herself. Sometimes she did.

Derek, who was the same age as me, didn't come to Silverlands until 1951 to join his brother and sister. The youngest of six, his three oldest siblings had been among those evacuated to America and all three had chosen to stay there. The other two, Pete and Madge, had been at Lennox Gardens during the war and were at Silverlands when Sue and I arrived. Derek, the baby of the family, was dragged around by his actor parents to dingy theatres and worse lodgings, sleeping on the end of his parents' bed, eating dreadful 'digs' food and, waiting in drafty dressing rooms in those small provincial theatres until the night's performance was over. By the time Derek was nine, when he arrived at Silverlands, he was painfully thin and asthmatic and thus he was fair game for a bully like Gordon. He frequently became his whipping boy. *I think about Derek's early years and am grateful that our mother spared us that life.*

One weekend – it must have been a weekend or in the summer because there was no school that day – Gordon told us to make sandwiches of our breakfasts (probably scrambled powdered eggs and bread). Then he took our sandwiches and put them into his Citroën and told us to walk to Virginia Water, a park about four miles away, telling us we were going on a picnic. When we arrived at *The Wheat Sheaf,* the pub by the park, he was there waiting for us and said he would give us back our breakfasts if we gave him our pocket money, which of course we didn't have with us. So off he drove, leaving us there, and we had to walk all the way home again, carrying the little ones piggyback; all of us tired, hungry and thirsty. Liz was eleven and Caroline and I were nine, that year. Many of the children were even younger than we were.

Gordon used to take some of the boys for a ride in his Citroën. As he drove and talked to the boys, he would, out of the blue, lose his temper and, with one hand on the steering wheel, he would turn around and start punching those boys in the back; all the while the car was careening around the lanes. The boys were terrified and thought they might die. Then Gordon would suddenly smile and say it was all a laugh. So the next time the boys would forget and want to go for a ride in his car again. *It sounds to me now as though he was possibly bipolar, although I doubt anyone knew what that was in those days.*

Brian said Gordon tried to turn the boys against Miss Berry and also encouraged them to tease the girls, just to please him and get in his good books. Some of them did.

It was while Miss Berry was headmistress, and before Gordon left, that Brian and a few of the older boys tried to run away. Walking to church one Sunday, they decided they would go to Kent. It was Leslie's idea and Kent was probably chosen because his family lived there. During the night, Leslie, his younger brother Michael, Brian, Peter and his brother

Derek raided the larder and quietly made their way on foot, down the driveway and walked in the direction that they thought would take them to Kent. There were no motorways in those days, just country roads and villages. Several hours later, they arrived in the outskirts of Staines, in quite the opposite direction from Kent. Tired, they rested for a while in a gravel pit. It was bitterly cold and very damp and Peter was concerned about his young brother Derek's wheezing. Disheartened, they decided to turn back. They arrived at Silverlands chilled to the bone, tired and late for breakfast.

Miss Berry gave them a stern talking to, probably with a lot of finger wagging and fat shaking, and sent them off to Frithwald and Stepgates, where they were also late. The Stepgates headmaster called Leslie, Brian and Peter into his office, one at a time, and gave them a caning for running away. *Teachers could do that in those days.* Somehow, Miss Berry always found someone else to do the hitting for her.

Ann remembered when the boys ran away and slept in the gravel pit. She said when they got back they told fantastic stories of their adventures, all probably highly exaggerated. She didn't know that they had been punished at Stepgates, she thought they had run away and were *never even* grounded. So Ann decided that she would run away to London and get a job. She got as far as Chertsey Station and was waiting for the train when she was caught and brought back. Afterwards, Miss Berry never let her forget it, constantly sneering at her. Sneering was something Miss Berry did well. She was continually reminding us how worthless we were and it was no wonder our parents didn't want us. *Those words made us feel very special indeed!*

One day, Pauline and Ann were alone in the 'Rec' room when Gordon came in. He told them that he suspected there was some 'hanky panky' going on between some of the boys and girls and that he knew some of the boys and girls were 'bedding together.' He brought his face very close to theirs and, in a menacing tone, demanded they tell him what they knew. They protested that they didn't know anything. Terrified, they backed away from him, but he kept walking straight at them, leaning into them. When they couldn't go any further and were up against the wall, Ann was sure Gordon was going to grab them. He screamed at them threatening vile punishment if they wouldn't tell him. They just kept stammering that they honestly didn't know anything. He went into a rage, stamped his foot and got very red in the face. Suddenly, he turned around and left the room. Some time later, Ann was walking down Holloway Hill by herself on her way to catch the bus to Guildford Day Commercial School. Gordon stopped her, grabbed her by the arm and snarled, "I'm taking you to a remand home for telling lies." Ann was petrified and kept begging him not to do that, but he just kept asking her over and over about the other kids and who was sleeping with whom. She managed to get away from him and ran as fast as she could for the bus.

This next Gordon story is mine. It was a Saturday in late summer and I was nine and a half. It must have been about four in the afternoon, because chores and games were over and I was to miss my tea. The day was sunny and warm and I wandered off alone, down Chestnut Avenue, just to hang about; to look at the rabbits in their hutches and maybe pick some flowers or find some good 'conkers.' I loved Chestnut Avenue and its trees with the pink and white blossoms every spring and wide spreading branches that were easy to climb. I could climb up into those leafy rooms and sit unseen, watching or reading.

We used to gather horse chestnuts and store them, like squirrels, until they hardened and were suitable for making a 'conker' by pounding a nail through the center, then threading an old shoelace or string through the hole and tying a big knot in the end. Once done, your 'conker' was ready for action. Next, you challenged someone . Wrapping the string around your fist, you held out your 'conker.' Your opponent would then whack yours with theirs. The game was over when somebody's nut got smashed. Sometimes you got your knuckles or wrists whacked instead. A champion 'conker' was one that had smashed many others. I had a niner once. But I digress.

On this Saturday, I was wandering down Chestnut Avenue when I saw a wisp of smoke coming from the field behind the trees. I moved closer to have a look. I had to climb through a prickly bush to get to the field and this wasn't easy because I was wearing a dumb skirt. We girls always wore skirts in those days and skirts were not at all conducive for hanging upside down from tree branches, though our navy blue knickers provided us with some modesty. I had been issued that particular skirt a week ago in my clean laundry bundle. It came from a charity shipment of second-hand clothing. The big girls sorted these clothes into sex and size, and then Matron gave us "new" clothes as we grew. This skirt was gray-blue and itchy and, as always, a little on the tight side, but it did have pockets and it was infinitely better than the last skirt I'd had, which had been an ugly bright green and much too small for me. I was also wearing a blouse, a liberty bodice and brown sandals with open toes. I wasn't wearing socks, which is how I know the day must have been fairly warm.

Anyway, I reached the smoke. There was a smoldering pile of leaves that the older boys must have raked together and burned earlier in the day. A ring of dirt had been cleared around the fire, to stop it spreading. The coals and embers were still hot, all orange and red, which made the leaves and sticks curl up as they burned; they made pictures like the scenery in Mother's plays. Every now and then grey bits of ashy leaves would float up in the smoke and into the air. I sat down cross-legged and stared into the fire, watching the pictures change and go from bright to dim. Wanting to make them change faster, I blew on it a bit and got up to fetch a stick. I began to poke the fire. I guess I must have been pretty engrossed in what I was doing because I didn't hear Mr. Gordon coming across the field. Before I knew what was happening, he had grabbed my right leg and stuck it into the embers. I screamed. My foot was getting really hot and it hurt a lot.

Gordon held my foot there for what felt like ages and said,

"Now Judy, this is what happens to little girls who play with fire. They get burned. This will teach you not to do it again."

He let go saying, "Run along in now and tell Matron to put something on that and then get down for tea. It you're late, you'll go without."

He strode off across the field to look for more children to torment.

I remember his words as if it was yesterday. I have often wondered about the make-up of a man who could be so matter-of-factly sadistic. He must have been psychotic. I hope he's dead. Brian said he was.

I stood there dumbly, well not dumbly, I was sobbing. (I had learned very young never to cry out loud – it only made them hit you harder). My foot hurt badly and red marks and blisters were beginning to show on my toes; the rubber sole had melted and was oozing up between them. I limped back up the field and across the driveway, through the courtyard, up the back door steps, along the back passage, then down the long main hallway and slowly up the stairs to Miss Rennie's dispensary.

"Well now, bairn," she said in her broad Scots accent, "What have you been up to"

"I burned my foot, Matron," I said.

"Let me look child," and she picked up my sore foot, "That's a nasty burn you've got there. We'll have to get the sandal off. How did you get that?"

"Mr. Gordon," I sobbed, "he pushed my foot in an old bonfire to teach me not to play with fire,"

"Hush child. You mustn't tell stories about Mr. Gordon. We won't say any more about it, shall we? We don't want to get into more trouble, do we? We don't want punishment to add to our misery, do we?"

She removed my sandal and tut-tutted. Then she put some yellow sticky ointment on my toes and, with gentleness and complicity, wrapped it all up in a big bandage.

"I think, young lady, you had better go straight to bed and stay off that foot for a day. I'll make sure that some tea is brought up to you, and I'll see that you're excused from church tomorrow. But promise me that you will never ever repeat that story about Mr. Gordon again. Promise me, child."

"Yes, Matron." I said.

And so I went to bed in my dormitory with the iron bedsteads and the lumpy horsehair mattresses and the big roses on the wallpaper that I counted at night when I couldn't sleep. And someone brought me a cup of tea and some bread with Marmite. Because of my burned foot, I was spared cold baked beans on toast and the long walk to church the next day. It has faded now, but I still have a bumpy scar across the three middle toes of my right foot.

Brian wrote many letters to me of his memories. This one about Gordon stands out:

At bath time, he would come in and stand there watching. If he felt like it, he would come over to some poor kid, usually he picked on one of the younger ones, and forced his head under water. We were all frightened of him. He also used to parade us up and down the passage in the nude. Then he would pick on one boy, force him down on the floor into a position so the boy couldn't move and start slapping the boy's face, pulling his nose and hair. He obviously enjoyed doing this in front of the rest of us, and if anyone moved, he would be next. He would usually do these things when the staff members were off duty or in Chertsey with the girls.

Then one day, he picked on Dave, a nice little boy with blond hair. We older boys watched helpless, while Bully Boy Gordon tormented Dave in front of the other little boys who were terrified. Poor Dave was screaming his head off, and there were no staff around to hear his cries for help. I was afraid too, but I couldn't stand it any longer. I remember jumping on Gordon and pulling him off little Dave. Then I took Dave's hand and we ran like hell and hid in a cupboard.

Later that evening when things were quiet, we crept back to our bedrooms. Gordon came into my room and tried to buy my friendship by offering me gifts. I told him what he could do with his gifts. He got angry and started punching me. In self-defense, I hit him back. Then I saw my chance and I made a run for it. I grabbed my coat, ran outside and across the field to the Hazell's bungalow. Mr. and Mrs. Hazell could see I was very upset. I told them about Gordon and what had been going on for some time, up at Silverlands.

Brian slept at the Hazells that night. Bert Hazell reported his story to the Orphanage authorities and shortly afterwards, Gordon was sacked.

Later that week, the older boys were walking home from school and Gordon was waiting in his car by the side of the road. He called them over. They went, unwillingly, always afraid. He said, "I have left Silverlands."

The boys ran home, excited and very relieved.

Everyone was glad when Gordon left. Brian was certain that *he* had got him the sack but I think most of us thought we had each helped Gordon get the sack. Pete claims that he did, and I thought I had, through Miss Rennie's intervention. But the Hazells had fostered Brian, and the Actors' Orphanage Fund had employed them for many years, (they had moved with the children from Langley Hall in 1938), so they were probably best able to convince the Committee that Mr. Gordon was a bad apple. Perhaps all the stories had a cumulative effect and they *had* to fire him.

In retrospect, our lot wasn't *always* bad. We gave as good as we got and while often the punishment didn't fit the crime, often it did. Many of the staff members were kind – bad apples are always the ones remembered. I'm sure that the labour pool available to the Actors' Orphanage Fund after the war, considering the wages they were able to pay, had pretty slim pickings. It probably listed many ex-army officers who were finding it hard to get employment elsewhere. *We* became their next boot camp. I know Mr. Duvall had been in the army in Burma, because I remember him telling us why it was unlucky to light three cigarettes on one match – he said that was how he lost his index finger, to a Japanese sniper. Aggitter's title of 'Commander' certainly implied recent service and given the dates he was with us, and his age, it is probably a sure thing that Gordon had once been a soldier.

The Committee, the London head office, and certainly our parents were probably unaware of these details in our daily lives. I knew, from harsh experience, that if you told your parent and he or she took your complaint to someone they knew on the Committee; they, in turn, would report the complaint to the headmaster, who would likely say the child was exaggerating or that the child got that welt from falling down – after all, it was his or her job on the line. If an under-master, such as Gordon, were the object of the complaint, he would be notified in turn by the head and warned to temper his actions. Eventually, of course, it would all come back to the child who had told a parent in the first place. Then he or she would *really* be in for it. We learned not to complain.

In 1981, when I first began to think about writing this memoir, after making some tentative enquiries, I received this letter from a former Committee member, Patrick Ide,

> My association with the Trust (Fund) only goes back about 27 years and it was not long after I joined that we decided that the Orphanage as such was an outmoded idea: so we disposed of it and took to subsidizing families of the children in need thus keeping family units together. I am sure that the committees and officers responsible for the Orphanage in earlier years were most responsible and dedicated people and kept in close touch with the well-being of those in their care: a tradition which is followed today. It is possible to criticize the general system of care, but it must be remembered that the Orphanage was only following the general pattern, believed in its time to be the best, and I am sure that the committee ensured that the care at that time was the best of the best available.

I, too, am sure their intentions were honorable, and indeed they did eventually address the way we were treated. My last six years were happier, and I hope no one is disturbed by these stories of our early years. They happened.

Shortly after Gordon was sacked in 1952, Miss Berry left under a cloud for her complicity. Patrick Waddington, appointed General Secretary to the Fund succeeding Miss Winnifred Rodda, began coming down on weekends. He also assumed the role of headmaster for a while until Alasdair Fraser, the handsome Scot who had come as housemaster to replace Gordon, was promoted the following year to headmaster. Things were looking up.

Father and Mother on their wedding day, January 1937

Father, Judy and Susannah, summer 1943

Susannah and Judy, 1945   My mother, Joan White c 1950

We Four: Judy, Sue, Liz
and Caroline 1947

Silverlands – the front door

Northeast corner

South view with air raid shelters

Chris, Pam, Carol, Peter, Brian, Charlie,
Michael, Gerry, Ed and Carl. 1950

Frithwald School: Triggy, Judy
and Susannah in front row, 1950

Christmas at Rutland Gate
(Sue is in paper hat kneeling),1952

Marlene, Noël Coward and the
children on the loggia, 1954

Noël Coward, Marlene Dietrich and Jonny, 1954

Miss Rennie, Mr. Fraser, Noël Coward, Doris,
Mr. Waddington and all of us, 1953

Judy, Gay and Ray with Mrs. Parker's
pekes and George the dog, 1956

Sir William Perkins School for Girls 3M, 1955

Home for the weekend: Peter,
Terry Mac and Gerry, 1957

Terry Mac
conducting, 1957

"Coke Squad": Carl,
Gerry and Mike, 1957

Granny and Grandad's house
in South Moreton

Liz and her friend Doreen at a Fancy Dress party
in the Assembly room, 1957

Richard Attenborough
at Open House, 1957

Gay, 1958

Confirmation, 1958 front row: Sarah, Gay, Margaret, Judy, Gaynor
rear: David Slater, Mike, Terry, Rev. Gardner, Kenny, Bernie

On the set of "Danger Within", 1958
with Richard Todd, Richard Attenborough and Vincent Ball

In my red Canadian parka
which Liz coveted, 1957

All the little girls in
the sand pit, 1958

Kirsten Slater with Lulu and Becky, 1957

Skegness on Sea,1958

Silverlands painted by Brian, and presented to
Lord Attenborough, September 2000

Former orphans and staff at the Reunion in Chertsey, September 2000

TEN

'Homes' for the Holidays

I USE THE word 'home' referring to Silverlands, because that is how I thought of it. I had lived there since I was very small, so to me Silverlands was my home. But I had other homes too: the houses where my relatives lived.

While our mother was still in England, Susannah and I usually travelled by train during our holidays to the repertory theatre where Mother was appearing, for a brief visit. We stayed at her invariably miserable 'digs', all three of us sleeping in the same sagging bed, and we ate smelly, unappetizing food prepared by the landladies. Salisbury was the exception, there Mother had two rooms in a lovely old house on the River Avon owned by a charming, eccentric and scholarly gentleman, Vivian McCann. Vivian had a cat called Da Poosey and he was not above re-laying his opinions about Mother's, sometimes garish, attire, by saying, "Miss White dear, Da Poosey thinks you look a teensy bit strange today." He was a kind man and Sue and I enjoyed Mother's engagements at the Salisbury Playhouse.

When we visited her, in those various repertory theatres around England, each night from the manager's box or from the wings we watched our Mother play smart ladies, drug addicts or Panto fairies and queens. With no one to leave us with, Sue and I went to every performance. It was the beginning of my theatrical education.

In Birmingham, we saw her play the Duchess of York to Alan Badel's *Richard III*. At Salisbury, in Jean Cocteau's *Les Parents Terribles* she played Yvonne, the drug-addicted mother, who dies a rather nasty death at the end. After the curtain fell, I ran backstage and sobbed to the stage manager, "What have you done to my mother?"

Mother was very flattered.

My happiest memory of those repertory days was at the Bristol Old Vic, the Christmas holiday I turned seven. The pantomime that year was *Puss In Boots*. Regular company members were always 'as cast' in the annual Panto. Mother was to play the Empress and dear 'Uncle' Newton Blick, the Emperor; both nice cameo roles. Lally Bowers, as Principal Boy, played the miller's youngest son and Donald Sinden and Donald Pleasance were his/her nasty brothers – this was quite some time before the West End, Broadway and Hollywood discovered them all. In one scene during the Panto, the Donalds would run through the audience with fully loaded water pistols and squirt the children.

One Friday, while Mother was queuing up to get her paycheck, Sue and I stood by her side plotting to buy some water pistols so we could fire back at the Donalds. We didn't know that Donald Sinden, also in the queue, had overheard us. That night, Sue and I were in the stalls, seated right on the aisle. We were sitting ducks. Donald and Donald came tearing off the stage and, before we could pull our water pistols out from under our bottoms, they were upon us and let us have it with both barrels. We stood up to return their fire, but their aim was better and they emptied their guns on us. Sue and I were thoroughly drenched and the audience loved it.

But generally speaking, visiting Mother at Birmingham, Salisbury, Bristol or Manchester, was mostly not really very glamorous or fun. During the day, the repertory theatres were dreary and cold, and re-hearsals were boring. Yet, sitting there in the evenings, when the house lights went down and stage lights came up, watching the scenes unfold – no matter what the play was – we were transported.

Sometime after we went to Silverlands, Mother had sold our Paultons Square house, in increasingly chic Chelsea, and in 1950 she bought an unassuming little three-story house near Regent's Park: Number Sixteen Linhope Street. She needed a base in London, between her repertory the-atre engagements, while she taught speech and drama at the R.A.D.A. and the London Central School of Speech and Drama or, when and if she was lucky enough to be cast in a West End production. While good parts for short character actresses were getting scarce, she did manage to get a few.

When she wasn't acting in Rep we sometimes stayed at 16 Linhope Street, but it was never home. The house was always full of lodgers, so Sue and I either shared an uncomfortable couch in the downstairs communal parlour or bedded down on the floor of Mother's bed-sitting room. For the extra income, Mother rented out every available room. Joan Sims lived there for several years, as did Inge and Berger Wilke, a nice Danish couple, and dear Laurena Dewar, Peter Eade's Scottish secretary. Peter Eade was Mother's agent whose clients also included Joan Sims, Ronnie Barker and Kenneth Williams. Peter had two of *the most* slobberous Boxer dogs and he would bring them over when we were visiting Mother. They romped with us, and slobbered on us, in her narrow backyard and we were sometimes allowed to take them for a walk in nearby Regent's Park.

16 Linhope Street was quite a comedown after Paultons Square. Behind the front parlour was a dark, ill-equipped kitchen and beyond that the only bathroom with a most temperamental geyser (hot water heater). With so many lodgers, it was rare to be able to have a bath in more than an inch of water and showers were unheard of then. There was also a small w.c., whose latched wooden door opened directly onto the backyard. A lot of rather risqué Victorian postcards were pinned to the door and sitting on the throne, legs dangling, I would stare at them and wonder what on earth those people were doing to each other.

Mother always told her friends and lodgers that Sue and I were home from 'boarding school'. I don't think that little white lie bothered me much in those days when I was small. Silverlands was my home and Mother was someone I visited. Someone rather glamorous, who was always very busy and seemed to pay attention to me with half an ear.

Until I was seven, I had an imaginary friend called Shirley. Staying at Linhope Street one holiday, my mother, who unlike her sister Audrey had no talent for cooking, admonished me to eat my carrots. I said, "Shirley's mother never makes her eat her carrots." Mother replied, "Shirley's mother should be spanked." On our next visit some months later, out of nowhere, Mother asked, "How is Shirley?" I replied brightly, "Oh, Shirley died."

I knew that Mother was part of my family, but Sue was much closer and, in truth, I *was* sad when she went to Rutland Gate. When Rutland Gate closed and just before Mother moved to Canada, Sue lived at 16 Linhope Street for six months or so, and slept on the couch. After we went to Silverlands in 1946, Sue and I never had a room of our own in *any* of our mother's homes.

Until I was about ten, I adored my mother from afar. To me, a chubby, bespectacled child, she was the very epitome of glamour. She always smelled wonderful and wore expensive clothes. My feelings started to change when one winter Sue and I were staying at Linhope Street after Christmas for a few days. Mother had been invited to a cocktail party. Sue and I had to go along. Sue willingly; I unwillingly. Sue was taking acting, dancing and singing lessons at school in London by then and she was very sure of herself in adult company. I was not. At the party, I stood near a large plant and tried to look inconspicuous. Sue socialized. Mother was chatting with a lady near my plant and I overheard the lady say,

"What a lovely child, your Susannah is, Joan dear. So poised and so pretty."

"Yes, isn't she." Mother said, "She's quite a handful, but she'll grow out of that."

"And how about little Judy?" asked the friend, "How will she turn out?"

"Oh," said Mother blithely, "I think Judy will be quite good looking when she's forty."

Forty! I thought I would die right there. When you're ten, at forty people have at least one foot in the grave, don't they? My adoration began to wane that evening.

In 1982, my first husband announced one night that, after eighteen years of marriage, he was leaving me for another woman. He was gone before breakfast. It so happened that my mother had been visiting us that weekend. After breakfast, still in a state of shock, I drove Mother to the bus. She rambled on, in the car, about her theatre school and her next play, completely unaware of my misery. I offered nothing.

Mercifully, the bus was on time. As she was getting on the bus, she turned to me and said sweetly, "Don't work so hard, dear."

One week later, still oblivious, she called to thank us both for such a lovely weekend. I told her he had left. The marriage was over. "Oh, dear," said she, "and he was such a lovely actor and so good-looking." I practically screamed into the phone, "Mother, I have two distraught daughters. Their father and I were married for over eighteen years. Have you nothing to say for me?"

"You're bloody lucky you had him that long," she rejoined, "Not one of my three marriages lasted more than seven."

By now I was furious. "Mother," I said, "When I was ten, I heard you tell someone that I'd be good-looking when I was forty. Well, I'll be forty in two months and I want you to know that I am a bloody knockout and I never want to speak to you again." I slammed down the phone.

It took me two years to be able to be civil to her, and only then because my eldest daughter was graduating from high school and leaving soon for college.

Usually during the school holidays Sue and I, and later just I, went to our grandparents' cottage, Wheatleys, in the village of South Moreton in Berkshire. They had a lovely little sixteenth century cottage with a pretty walled garden and, happily for Granddad, it was next door to the pub. Sue and I had our very own bedroom, upstairs underneath the sloping roof. There we had our own beds and even a bookcase for our books. Each morning, Sue and I would lean out of the little latticed casement window and watch the cows walking through the village on their way to pasture. We loved it there.

Until I was eleven, after Sue had left Silverlands, if I was going to visit my grandparents, I was put on the train at Chertsey Station and met by Miss Rodda, and later Mr. Waddington, at Waterloo Station. From there I was escorted to Paddington station and put on another train. I had a label pinned to my coat and I was put 'in charge of the guard'. The label said my name, my grandparents' address and *'Please put this child off at Didcot.'* Most of the time the guards were nice men and let me ride in the guards' van with the luggage, where they gave me chocolate Digestive biscuits and tea from their thermos flasks. Some would point out the sights from the train – Peek Frean's Biscuit Company in Reading was a remembered highlight.

After I turned twelve, I was on my own. Granddad always met the train at Didcot in his green Morris with its comfy familiar smells of leather seats, tobacco and his old, brown tweed jacket. As he drove along the narrow country roads to South Moreton, we talked about what we were going to do while I was there: we could have a picnic on the Wittenham Clumps; or, for a treat, go down to Henley to watch the sculling on the Thames, having lunch at the Shillingford Bridge Hotel on the way; and we always drove into Wallingford on Market Day. But, he never once asked me about Silverlands or school, I think he was embarrassed that I had to be there. He, Granny and Audrey never came to Silverlands, not once, in all the years I lived there. But he was a kind man though rather formal in some ways. He used to send Sue and I Valentine cards every year signed "sincerely, H.W.G. White." Sue used to pretend they were from a boyfriend, without much success.

When asked, my grandfather was a fount of information about all sorts of things. He told me about growing up in Somerset and Devon where his father and grandfather were solicitors and magistrates; about his great-uncle General William George White who had served in far-off India and was there during the Indian Mutiny in 1857; and about his five maiden aunts Ellen, Emily, Louise, Henrietta and Mary. He told me about his schooldays at All Hallows School in Honiton, Devon and about his younger sisters, but he would never *ever* talk about his mother. Emma Lee Byron Harril was a half Romany girl who had left his father, himself and his little sisters when he was only eight. Brought up by those five spinster aunts, it is no wonder that at sixteen he went to sea as a cabin boy on the trans-Atlantic cable-laying ships of the Eastern Telegraph Company.

Always stressing the importance of hard work and stick-to-itiveness, he told me how he had worked his way up through the ranks and, as a young man in the late1890s, had been posted to the remotest islands in the Atlantic to man the cable stations, hooking up the great spools of cable when the ships arrived from Europe or, attaching new spools to take the cables on to the Americas. On St. Helena, Tristan da Cunha, Ascencion and Bermuda, he and some twenty other men lived and worked for nine months straight, followed by three months home leave. With not much to do, in such isolation, they taught themselves to knit, to hook rugs and make string hammocks. He could tie any kind of knot (and he taught me a few). The men played many different card games, cribbage, chess and draughts and they would recite to each other their favorite poems – Grandad could still recite *The Boy Stood on the Burning Deck* when he was eighty-five – or Music Hall numbers, and the names of things: birds, flowers, shells, fish and the stars. My grandfather passed a lot of that knowledge and lore on to me. He taught me how a car engine worked, how to take a bicycle apart and, most importantly, how to change a flat tyre.

At thirty, home on leave, he met my grandmother. She was the seventh and youngest child of a prominent Salisbury cutler and, at twenty-seven, was verging on spinsterhood for those days. They married, had two daughters, and lived together happily for almost sixty years. In South Moreton, I learned much that I didn't learn at Silverlands.

Grandfather's life revolved around his weekly, highly secretive Masonic meetings (about which the women of his family were told nothing) and his cronies at the pub next door. Granny would to send me to The Crown to fetch him, and I, standing on the Watneys floor mat outside the taproom, would say, "Please may Bunny White come home for supper now?" Then he and I, seventy-seven and ten, would teeter across the car park, unlatch the green gate to Granny's little rose garden, open the front door and he would call out, "We're home, Kay." A life-long smoker, he stood in that little rose garden every morning, coughing and coughing. Much later, I found out that he smoked unfiltered Turfs and Woodbines, instead of the milder Players, because I was collecting the cigarette cards.

When he was a very old man, after my aunt Audrey had moved them back to the warmer climate of Gibraltar, Granddad lost his senses of taste and smell completely. (As a diabetic he was not supposed to drink any alcohol – but he always did!) Once they were settled in Gibraltar,

Audrey kept a whiskey bottle half-filled with cold tea in the kitchen and Granddad would sneak drinks from it and get drunk as a lord.

Granny liked her little nip, too, which she always said was medicinal. While Granddad was at The Crown or in Wallingford with the Masons, after her chores were done Granny would pour herself a small glass from her supply of gin in the Welsh dresser, sit down and listen to *Housewives Choice, Worker's Playtime,* or the *BBC Women's Hour.* They both tuned in daily to *The Archers, Mrs. Dale's Diary* and Granddad especially loved, 'ancock's 'alf 'our.* He would lie back in his armchair by the fire in his brown waistcoat, jacket off, with a large linen handkerchief over his face, chuckling until he fell asleep.

Granny was a tireless volunteer for the Women's Institute, for South Moreton's ancient Norman church, and she also had a very green thumb. Every morning Farmer Hedges' cows went through the village, and every morning out would go Granny with her bucket and spade to scoop up the cow plop for her garden of fruits, flowers and vegetables. Between the cow manure and the large compost heap at the back, where Chat the cat sunned himself, Granny's garden never lacked for nutrition. When ripe, the cabbages and beets, apples, loganberries and damson plums were stored, alongside the milk, meat, butter and cheese, in her north-facing larder, its window covered with wire mesh not glass. Refrigeration was only for the wealthy in South Moreton, in the nineteen fifties.

When Sue was with me for the holidays, we used to lie on our stomachs for hours trying to catch minnows in jam jars from the little stream behind the Crown or have snail races on the roof of Grandad's tool shed. We held elaborate funerals for any dead creature we found: mice, baby birds and once a dead cat from the farm; the ground under the pear tree had many wonky wooden crosses and flat stone markers. Some days, we'd walk through the field, put a ha'penny or a farthing on the railway track and, when we heard the train in the distance, we'd scamper up to the bridge to wave at the engine driver. Then, we'd run down to the tracks and get our flattened coins once the train had passed.

We became friendly with Gilly and Anne, the Squire's daughters at the Hall, the biggest house in the village, where the Hedges family lived and farmed. It was right across the road from Gran's house. We played croquet on their big lawn or we hung about the farm when there were new baby animals to see. The Hedges used to have fancy dress garden parties and we were always invited. Although I was shy it was an event not to be missed, and I was once persuaded to wear a Simple Simon-Pie man's outfit and carry a tray of little nibbles around to the guests.

Sometimes, after Sue and Mother had gone to America, I invited a friend from Silverlands to come with me to South Moreton: someone who wasn't as lucky and didn't have a Granny and Granddad or an Aunt Audrey. I asked Gaynor once, and Gay twice, but Gay was such a city girl and she didn't really enjoy rambling across fields looking for wild-flowers and birds' nests. It seemed contradictory to her very nature when, years later, she became the wife of a Welsh sheep farmer, for she was such a Londoner through and through.

My aunt Audrey lived just a mile away from her parents – and a world away from her older sister. She could be crusty, often with reason, but she had a heart of gold and I loved her dearly.

While I was in South Moreton, I was given an old blue three-speed bicycle; a Raleigh. As a teenager, I would take a book, an apple and a sandwich and go off for the day – free as a bird – to lie in some open field and read. One summer day, I got back very late, having fallen asleep, and my aunt, who I knew loved me, slapped me hard across the face and said I was never to be late again, I had made her worried sick. It hurt that I had worried her, much more than the slap.

Audrey lived in North Moreton where she ran Colliers Universal Worm Drive Hose Clip factory from a converted manor house and lived upstairs with her cats, Gina, Carlos and Mattie. Michael Collier owned the factory. He had invented the eponymous hose clips which had proved invaluable during the war, holding together various important parts of aeroplanes, ambulances and other military vehicles. 'Uncle' Michael profited greatly, both from his invention and from my aunt, who not only ran his factory but also served as his hostess and mistress for twenty years. She cooked for him, took care of his daughter when she was home from boarding school and, in the dark of night, would run silently across the lawn to his house, so the neighbours wouldn't know. Of course they knew, everybody knew; Michael and Audrey went on holiday together every year, touring Europe in his big grey Bentley and sampling five star restaurants.

Audrey was a wonderful cook. She made us huge, mouth-watering meringues covered in a chocolate sauce that neither Sue nor I have ever been able to duplicate. I can see her now, an apron over her clothes, a cigarette dangling from her mouth, standing over the Aga in her espadrilles cooking a Spanish *zarzuela*, a French *coq au vin* or creating some other dish out of whatever was in the larder, often at a moment's notice. One time, Michael was to come for Sunday dinner and Audrey had planned to make a salmon Florentine. To her dismay, she discovered that she had fed the tinned salmon to the cats by mistake and all she had in the larder was tinned cat food. Being Sunday, of course the village shop was shut. Undaunted, she opened the cat food cans, added various herbs, a little wine and cream, and laid it all over a bed of fresh spinach from her garden. Michael never knew what he was eating. He declared it "simply delicious!"

When Michael's wife, who hadn't lived with him for years, died and he was finally free to marry again, that rotter tossed Audrey aside and married another woman. Unlucky in love twice, her first husband was killed in the war, she moved with her aging parents to Gibraltar and, after they died, moved deep into the hills of Spain and lived like a native when Franco closed the border. She took to drink, drank too much and, after many years, died of alcohol poisoning in the *loca* ward of a Spanish hospital. I was with her when she died. I miss her still.

There was a reason that our grandparents and Audrey didn't take Sue and I, when Mother needed somewhere to put us. By 1946, Granny and Grandad were in their seventies and not physically able to take care of two little girls and, Audrey had her job and her man. However, Sue and I were luckier than some of our fellow orphans because, in South Moreton Audrey, Granny and Granddad made us feel we were part of a family.

In order that every child should have a summer holiday, for two weeks every August the Actors' Orphanage Fund rented rooms in a seaside town. Sue and I always went on these holidays. In the early fifties, we went to Selsey Bill, Bournemouth and Bexhill-on-Sea. I went with the

Slaters to Broadstairs, Margate and, in our last year, to Skegness, a cold and windy place on the North Sea.

Ann in Australia wrote to me about her memories of those annual summer holidays,

> Mr. Cullum was the owner of the house where we stayed in
> Selsey. It was quite a big house and had an arch in the garden
> with a pear tree growing over it; smallish, brownish pears. I think
> we all went there again the next year. Then, after that we went
> to Bexhill where Pauline and I hung out of a window talking
> to a couple of local boys and later we sneaked out, went for a
> walk with them and I had my first ever snog. Silverlands had a
> rather glamourous young au pair named Marianne, that year.
> She used to wake the older ones up at 6 a.m. each day and take
> us to the beach. She would do handstands and back flips on the
> beach and her elasticized costume would frequently fall down
> and expose her tits, which was the highlight of each morning!

[Liz, reading over my shoulder when I wrote this, interjected that Marianne also did this on the grass between the air-raid shelters back at Silverlands – not in a bathing dress, but in a skirt with frilly knickers underneath. "She must have got a sexual buzz out of it," said Liz.]

Ann again,

> The last summer I was there, 1954, we went to a house in
> Southbourne, near Bournemouth. There weren't enough
> bedrooms, so the boys all slept in the garden in a couple of tents,
> which we girls visited whenever we got the chance. I remember
> Miss Rennie was with us there, and she took her nephew
> David along, he was a year older than me. I had a huge crush
> on him and had my second snog. Long time between snogs.

From Silverlands, Sue and I always had family to go to after Christmas, at Easter and in the summer. And, almost always, someone came to take us out on Visiting Sundays. After our Orphanage seaside holiday, Sue and I, and later just I, went a few times to Auntie Vi and Auntie Chris at

Sea Pines in Milford-on Sea. They, who had kindly taken us in the year before Mother found Silverlands.

Some children never went anywhere beside those seaside holidays, and many of them were the ones who waited in vain for a parent or *someone* to come on Visiting Sundays. Terry Mac was one of those children. He told me, years later when I stayed with him in London, about the Adoption Parades. Growing up I never knew about them, and I am sure our mother would never have consented for us to be adopted, but on looking back it explains why some children came, stayed a few months and, without any explanation, were gone rather abruptly. Terry Mac said on certain days he was told to put on his Sunday clothes and go to the front hall. There some strangers, along with a committee member or two, would inspect him and a few other kids. Some time later, one of those children would be gone; adopted by a kindly couple? Terry Mac was never chosen. When he was telling me about those Adoption Parades, he said how much they had undermined his self-esteem and affected the way he lived as an adult.

> *Of all the boys at Silverlands, I was fondest of Terry Mac and I stayed in touch with him over the years. He worked in the theatre for a while and was a house manager at the National Theatre the last time I stayed with him in 1982. He'd already had one divorce by then and a couple of difficult relationships. Eventually, he married Monica and they moved to Devon where they had two sons. His last years were happy, but he died much too young at fifty-two, in 1991, of a heart attack.*

My sister and I were more wanted than unwanted. We had our grandparents and aunt to stay with during our holidays; we had those occasional 'aunts' and 'uncles', Mother's friends where we stayed for brief visits; Aunty Monica and Uncle Arthur (our father's brother) occasionally invited us to their home in nearby Wimbledon and, for Visiting Sundays until 1954 we had our mother, who always did come down on Visiting Sundays, *if she wasn't working*.

Visiting Sunday was the third Sunday of the month. After lunch, parents arrived, in taxis from Chertsey station, in hired cars or in cars belonging to their current paramours. Our mother would invariably arrive on the arm of some man. She was always dressed smartly, lightly perfumed with *Je Reviens*, and wearing a stylish hat at a rakish angle on her beautifully waved hair, a little fox tippet slung around her shoulders. Her gentlemen friends, usually actors or writers, wore country tweeds, spoke in resonating tones and smelled of a careful mixture of tobacco and expensive aftershave lotion. Up the drive they would come in a smart touring car, greet us dramatically and hand us into the rumble seat. Susannah and I would sit in the back, slightly nauseated from the petrol and perfumes.

Mother would talk too loudly and *act* maternal. She took credit for our manners (we were usually embarrassed and silent), our dresses (hand-me-downs ironed by Matron for the occasion) and our looks (genetically hers). We would be taken to the Chertsey Bridge Hotel on the River Thames and be treated to tea and cakes and sometimes (heaven oh heaven!) Walls Ice Cream. After an awkward hour or so, with maybe a walk along the towpath, and once in a punt on the river with one of her nicer beaus, we would be returned to Silverlands until the next month. Sometimes, due to her engagements, Mother would be unable to come. Then we would stay at Silverlands and watch for other parents to arrive, and feel for those kids whose parents said they would come but never did. Ann's mother was like that and so was Norma's. At least *we* knew when our mother wasn't coming, and she did always come when she said she would.

On one of the days that Mother couldn't come, Triggy's mother came down with Herbert Lom and they invited Liz and me to have tea with them at Chertsey Bridge. We were so excited. Of course, we didn't know then that he was really famous, but we did notice that people came up and asked for his autograph.

Liz has asked me, "Do you think Triggy's mother and Lom were having an affair? She was really good-looking, actually she was beautiful."

Triggy came to Silverlands in 1950 and stayed three or four years. She was Liz's age, a little older than me. At the time, her mother was a light opera singer appearing in either works by Gilbert and Sullivan or Ivor Novello. Triggy would usually be singing either *Three Little Maids from School are We* or *Overhead the Moon is Beaming,* depending on her mother's current engagement.

After Sue and Mother had gone to America, I usually went alone for holidays with my aunt and grandparents. Once, I went with Liz to her father and stepmother's flat in Camden Town. Another time, I stayed at Gay's mother's flat in Eccleston Square after Gay had visited South Moreton and, just the once, I spent a remembered long weekend at the home of Sir Frederick and Lady Hooper at their country estate, The Dandy, in Tenterden, Kent.

Prudence Hooper was a former actress who had once worked with Mother and then married well. She and Mother had remained friends and, as a favour to Mother after she'd gone to Canada, she invited me to spend a weekend and be company for her small daughter, Emma. I was twelve and Emma was five! Emma lived mostly with her nice nanny on the nursery floor of The Dandy. We were an awkward pairing, Emma and I, since I was past the age where I dipped toast 'soldiers' into my soft-boiled egg and wasn't good at playing with dolls – I had never had a doll, just Sue's old Teddy.

Sir Frederick, a one-time barrow boy, was the President of Schweppes, Inc. 'Uncle Freddy' was a lovely man and very kind to me. So were Nanny and Richard, the Jamaican butler – the first black man I ever saw.

'Aunty' Prue was another story. She made me feel quite the poor relation, which I suppose I was. She insisted that I learn to play Whist with her and, at dinner, which I was permitted to attend, she corrected my orphanage table manners, saying, "Judy dear, when you come out, you *will* need to know which fork to use." *When I come out, indeed! As if I would ever do such a thing!*

Fast-forward twenty years. My first husband and I with our two small daughters were visiting London before going on to Scandinavia. Mother had written to, the now widowed, Lady Hooper that I was coming to England and so she invited us, all four of us, to tea at The Connaught Hotel. I was a little nervous, but was bolstered by my pretty girls and my well spoken, Harvard educated, handsome husband. We arrived to find her in the lobby swathed in furs and

slightly tipsy. We went into tea and took our places at a table. The
children behaved perfectly, my husband was charming and she seemed
quite disappointed that I hadn't married some lout who picked his teeth
at table and belched. When we left, my husband remarked, "What a
dreadful snob!"

Later, when we learned that Emma had run away from home and
married a Lebanese businessman, Sue and I both said, "Way to go,
Emma!"

On Visiting Sundays, after Sue and Mother had gone, I was taken
out, rather reluctantly on my part, by Mother and Audrey's middle-aged
bachelor cousins to spend afternoons with my ancient great-aunts in
nearby Woking. Macklin Stratton and Adrian Beach were my second
cousins once removed. Macklin, an ear, nose and throat specialist at
Guys Hospital lived with his mother, Great Aunt Ethel, Granny's sister,
in Woking. Macklin was something of an amateur historian and knew
all about the history of Silverlands and the surrounding area. History was
my favorite subject at school and I enjoyed his stories. A bit of a dry old
stick and probably unused to the ways of awkward adolescents, he drove
me to their small house and there, Aunt Ethel, who always slept in long-
dead Great Uncle Percy's long underwear every night, would make us a
lunch of undercooked chops and burned peas. When Aunt Ethel finally
died, Mack surprised everyone by marrying a rather eccentric, but great
fun, lady artist, and he and his Joan promptly adopted two children.

Sometimes Adrian took me out instead., Adrian was a gentle soul
who lived in Mayford with his mother, my Great Aunt Lucy. Aunt Lucy
was rather Bohemian and much more energetic than Great Aunt Ethel.
She and I would go for bicycle rides, gathering windfalls from apple
trees we passed and taking them home to make pies. "Waste not, Want
not!" was her favorite saying. I had fun with Aunt Lucy and was sad
when she died. Adrian was an artist: a very respected landscape painter
– a member of the Royal Academy! He had a wealthy patron who paid
for him to spend winters in the Mediterranean, painting Roman ruins
and Spanish gypsies. After his indefatigable mother died, Adrian hired

a local woman to come in and 'do' for him. When Adrian died, Macklin wrote to me in America,

> I am quite at a loss as to what to do. I have learned
> that the good woman, who was taking care of Adrian,
> had been folding his lovely sepias and watercolours *in
> half* and tidying them away in a chest of drawers."

I wonder if Adrian ever knew. He was always in another world. But I was lucky to have these older cousins who took the time to care.

ELEVEN

The Winds of Change 1953-55

BY THE END of 1952, Miss Berry and Mr. Gordon had been dismissed and, Patrick Waddington, a once and future actor, replaced Miss Winnifred Rodda as General Secretary. Temporarily he lived at Silverlands as nominal Headmaster, in addition to his duties in London, to make sure that no further terrors were visited upon us.

Upon assuming his duties, he had immediately made it clear to the Committee that the Fund had not invested in essential equipment to make the Orphanage run properly; that there was low staff morale (one of the more recent matrons had suffered a nervous breakdown – probably poor Wiggy Williams); that the general administration of Silverlands was all wrong; and that staffing on certain levels was dangerously inadequate.

Well, we'd had rather a lot of short-term staff for quite some time. I expect some of them left when they found they couldn't work under Miss Berry. Anyway, now that Miss Berry and Mr. Gordon were exposed and gone for good, Mr. Waddington set about hiring staff he could trust. When he was not in residence, we were now in the *verra* capable hands of two Scots, Miss Rennie and Alasdair Fraser.

Possibly in reaction to Gordon's recent reign of terror, Mr. Fraser had tentatively suggested to Mr. Waddington that *only* in cases of gross disobedience, cruelty or beastliness, would the smaller boys be most effectively dealt with by some physical chastisement administered at once. Mr. Waddington asked for instruction from the Committee. After some lengthy discussion, it was stated in the minutes of a meeting in July 1952 that,

> Mr. Fraser could exercise his discretion but
> should keep any physical chastisement restricted
> to small boys and to a minimum of cases.

At an earlier meeting, both Miss Jill Esmond and Mr. Waddington had expressed grave concern over the problem of enabling the girls be escorted to and from the bus stop during the dark winter months. The uncomfortable proximity of the Botleys Mental Home was mentioned. Their concern was probably because, on two occasions, unsavory men in small dark cars had lured girls to their open car windows, on the pretext of asking a simple question, and then exposed themselves.

Poor Liz was subjected to two such 'sightings.' The first one involved herself and Caroline on the way home from Frithwald one day. A man had been sitting in a small dark car in a lay-by on the side of the road. He beckoned them over to ask directions and when they got to his window, his flies were open. They backed away. When they got home, they reported it to Mr. Fraser. The police came and Liz and Caroline were driven around in a police car trying to spot the man or his car, with no luck.

Later, after a man matching their description was arrested, Caroline had to go to court to testify. The magistrate asked her, "Tell us what the man was doing."

Caroline, who was always very shy, was tongue-tied.

So a policewoman asked her gently, "Was the man was stroking his penis, dear?" and Caroline whispered, "Yes."

The second time was a little while later. Liz and I were walking along Lyne Lane. It was a Sunday and we were headed for church and lagging behind the others. A dark-green car was parked across the road, a man sitting in the driver's seat. He seemed to be looking at a map. He called us over. We were polite little girls, so we went. He wasn't reading a map!

"Hello little girls," he said, "Have you ever seen one of these before?" Liz, who had been through this already and besides hadn't we both grown up with lots of boys and seen it all, said quickly, "Yes we have and we're late for church. Come along, Judy." She grabbed my hand and pulled me away.

I was quite stupefied. I had only seen the boys' private parts, and they looked like little pink sausages, this man's was certainly different – different and creepy. We ran to catch up with the other kids and told them about it, but the church bell was ringing. The man was gone by the time we walked home. We did tell Miss Rennie, but I don't think anything further was done.

Berry and Gordon having left under dark clouds, Mr. Waddington's clean sweep was possibly instigated by Noël Coward, who had noted, ominously, in his diary earlier on 29 August 1952,

> Long serious discussion about the Orphanage. Decided to make drastic economics – sell Silverlands and get somewhere near London where the Hostel can be under the same roof. If we don't do something soon we shall have exhausted our capital in a few years and have to close down. Much as I would like to resign, I cannot do so until the whole thing is properly solvent.

Clearly, Coward was frustrated. He must have been upset to find that the Savage-Baileys' replacements were a hundred times worse and things at Silverlands were in a sorry state, both physically and financially.

Happily, the following year *Night of a Hundred Stars* was born at the Palladium and some of the financial worries were over, for a while. The first *Night of a Hundred Stars* made a clear profit of no less than ten thousand pounds – one night at the Palladium had made more money for the Actors' Orphanage than all the years of Theatrical Garden Parties put together! Night of a Hundred Stars, the bright idea of Charles Russell and Lance Hamilton, was to bring together on the stage of the Palladium, for one night only, all the stars of stage and screen currently available in London. And they didn't just get the stars to commit, but put them together in the most unlikely acts: Dame Edith Evans with Hermione Gingold; Vivien Leigh, Laurence Olivier, Danny Kaye and John Mills in a musical number; Tyrone Power singing and dancing with a bevy of chorus girls, each one of them a well-known actress, to the delight of the audience. The lighting, sound and stage-management of the Palladium staff all came up trumps. Coward felt immense gratitude and great relief – there was no reason why the show should not be repeated every year and the Actors' Orphanage could, after all, survive financially.

The show was produced annually until 1957, raising much-needed funds. I only went to the last one, but I had heard about the earlier shows. It must have been great fun to watch Laurence Olivier doing a

Top Hat number with John Mills, and Bob Hope cutting in to waltz with Olivier.

There were many other occasions when generous members of the theatrical profession contributed to the upkeep of the Orphanage. Emlyn Williams donated the proceeds of the October 9, 1950 performance of his play, *Accolade,* to the Fund. In April 1953, producer Emile Littler bettered that offer and gave one whole week of profits from his smash hit *Love From Judy,* the musical comedy based on Jean Webster's novel *Daddy Longlegs.* I felt a deep personal attachment to this show, after we all went by motor coach to London to see Jean Carson as Judy – the little orphan girl.

Some of us – those who were old enough – went up to London again to sell programmes at a matinee performance. Feeling small and rather shabby in our hand-me-down dresses and sensible shoes, Janet and I stood, clutching a stack of programmes, at the top of an aisle in the orchestra section of the Saville Theatre as we timidly asked mink-clad matinee ladies, "Excuse me, madam, would you like to buy a souvenir programme?" Some ladies were kind and smiled at us as they paid the one shilling and sixpence, but I remember to this day those, who curtly said, "Certainly not." And one woman, in particular, saying loudly as she tottered down the aisle on her high heels, "Really, the impertinence of selling programmes to support those illegitimate brats on top of these exorbitant ticket prices."

Why do the mean words always stay with you? I had only recently heard my own mother say, "I expect Judy will be good-looking when she's forty." And by saying those few words, she ensured that I felt ugly, homely, fat, four-eyed and totally unappealing.

Patrick Waddington was an on-the-spot administrator. He came down almost every weekend on his motor scooter. His chosen room was at the end of our corridor, between the older girls corner room and Miss Rennie's dispensary. Two of the senior girls, Ann and Pauline had to ready the room for his arrival each time. They were full of admiration about how he had arranged the room so that his bed was diagonally placed in the very centre of the floor and covered with many fancy quilts. He hung colorful draperies at the window and the walls were covered with arty pictures and large personal photographs: some of him appearing in plays and some from his Air Force days. Before he came to Silverlands, between 1926 and 1950 he had been a working actor and had appeared in many plays and films.

We came to know him quite well, unlike his predecessor Miss Rodda who had rarely made an appearance at Silverlands. With the advent of Mr. Waddington came two wonderful dogs, George and Malcolm. They were nothing at all like Miss Berry's obese Golden Retriever or the Aggitter's rutting Jack Russell terrier, they were friendly, happy dogs and they seemed to belong to all of us, not just to Mr. Waddington. Many of us wept when a car on Lyne Lane killed Malcolm. He'd been with us for only a year or two, but George lived on to a ripe old age.

On weekends, Mr. Waddington took us for walks – well, more like forced marches. He was a tall man and he rather fancied himself in his country costume: tweed jacket and plus fours tucked into Argyle socks worn with proper leather walking shoes. He would set the pace and we all followed, puffing and panting behind him, trying to keep up with his long strides. On these walks, he would frequently question those walking nearest to him about schoolwork or encourage us all to sing marching songs: *One Man Went to Mow* or *Be Kind to your Web-footed Friends*. And it seemed he was always there on Sundays, to walk with us to church.

It didn't take very long for him to take against the uninspiring Vicar Hodge at Lyne Church and so, sometime in 1953, our religious allegiance was transferred to Ottershaw parish, three miles along the Guildford Road. Ottershaw's Christ Church was set on a hill above the village. I don't remember if the Vicar there was any better than Vicar Hodge, but the church wasn't nearly as gloomy inside and had many pretty stained-glass windows and lots of memorials to read during the sermons. But Ottershaw was at least two miles further than Lyne and, since we always walked almost everywhere we went, it was quite a trudge.

Every Sunday morning for two years, we put on our clean clothes issued the night before, formed a crocodile and walked behind Mr. Waddington, nattily attired in his plus fours, Oxford gown and mortar board – three miles there and three miles home. When we stumbled to a halt at *The Otter*, the local pub at the bottom of the hill, Mr. Waddington, or 'Prod' as we called him behind his back, would call out in ringing tones, "Do any of you wish to relieve yourselves?" Well, of course, we *all* did. *That poor publican must have dreaded Sunday mornings.*

As an actor and ex-Oxonian, Mr. Waddington was invariably called upon to read the lesson, which he did in his beautifully modulated, RADA-trained voice. With his military bearing, high forehead (on account of receding grey hair), splendidly groomed mustache and theatrical sense of dress, he was a most imposing figure at the lectern for those lowly parishioners of Ottershaw.

> *As children, we made fun of his style of dress and his actor-ish ways, but I now know he was a kind man who did his job well and had our welfare at heart. He left in 1956, after 'coming a cropper' on his motor scooter and having to be hospitalized. When he recovered he returned to acting, appearing in the film* A Night to Remember. *By 1959, he was in America, touring as Leicester in* Mary Stuart. *When I was working in the theatre in New York in the early 1960's, so was he. He came to see me act in* The Saving Grace *and* The Magistrate *and I returned the compliment and saw him play featured roles in* Rosmersholm *and* Kean, *and also when, as understudy, he went on for Cyril Ritchard in* The Pleasure of His Company. *He was really quite good. He invited me to cocktail parties at his apartment in Greenwich Village on a number of occasions and there, he treated me as an equal. He went back to England in 1964 and, after doing a few West End roles and a couple of episodes of television as The Brigadier in* Dad's Army, *he retired to York where he was born. He died there in 1984.*

I remember two occasions when Mr. Waddington took some of us rather firmly in hand. While he never laid a hand on us, he gave some rather effective, corrective demonstrations. One had to do with stealing. Like many kids, we went through a period of minor shoplifting or 'finders-keepers.' Someone had been caught red handed by the manager of Woolworth's in Chertsey stealing a small Matchbox car. Mr. Waddington called us together and, when he had our attention, he took some change out of his pocket. He laid a ha'penny on the table:

"First, it is this," he said.

Next he laid a threepenny bit on the table, "Then it is this."

Then he put down a shiny half-crown. "Soon, it will be this and, before you know it, it will be this."

With a flourish he drew out a roll of paper money – ten shilling-, one pound-, and even five pound notes. Our eyes bugged out.

He said, "When you steal something small and get away with it, the temptation is to steal more and, eventually, you'll end up in jail. So I am warning you, stop now."

His other practical demonstration had to do with smoking. The boys had all, at one time or another, tried smoking. Sometimes they rolled their own out of dried leaves and exercise book paper, other times someone stole a cigarette a staff member had left lying around or picked up a half smoked butt. Brian saved his pocket money to buy a packet of ten for about ten pence (in those days). He would then sell individual cigarettes for threepence each and soon sold out. He had a tidy little business going. One Saturday afternoon, Waddington invited the early smokers into his sitting room. He put down on the table several packets of cigarettes: Turf, Woodbines, Dunhills, Players Navy Cut, and several boxes of Swan Vestas matches. Everybody was invited to light up. They did. Pretty soon, after a few cigarettes, everyone was running outside to cough and throw up. *It was a good lesson, but I don't think it stuck.*

In 1953 and 1954, there were many new arrivals at Silverlands. *Lucky them for having missed Gordon!* Margaret and her younger brothers, Ronnie and Graham, arrived; Frank, who stayed just a short while, before he was adopted; two brothers, James and Andrew, lived with us for just a few years until their actor father got back on his feet financially. Louis and his younger brother Val came, cousins of Terry Mac and Paddy, their parents were running a theatre in South Africa. The parents later divorced and after their mother remarried, she took the boys and their little sister Siobhan to live with her. Siobhan was only with us for our very last year. Val eventually immigrated to Australia with his mother and stepfather and the family adopted young Norma whose own mother had abandoned her. Siobhan like her brother, Louis, ended up in Canada. Louis became a guitarist playing in clubs with various bands in London before moving to Canada where he formed the rock band, *Influence,* in the late 1960s.

Norma had arrived at Silverlands, in late 1951, only four years old. Her mother was forever promising to come on Visiting Sundays but she never ever did. Poor Norma sat on those front steps all Sunday long, year in and year out, waiting for her mother – who never came!

Lally, a year older than Norma, arrived a year later when she was six. Then came Jennifer who, according to Ann, had a doting Mum who wrote to her daily. I don't remember Jennifer very well; she must not have stayed very long. Indeed, if she was there during the reign of 'Bully Boy' Gordon, that doting Mum probably took her away – quickly. Some children only lived with us for a very short time before returning to their parents, who had either remarried or landed a lucrative job. For those children, Silverlands was just a stopgap, a place for children from theatrical families when times were hard.

Long-legged Gaynor, with almost as many Christian names as Royalty and her olive complexion, arrived around in 1953 and not long after her came Gay and her little brother Bill. Gay was to become my closest friend, eventually joining me at William Perkins Grammar School for Girls. She and I stayed in touch long after we had both left Silverlands and moved on. Both Gay and Gaynor joined Margaret, Caroline, Janet and I in the largest dormitory for the next couple of years. And there was Mavis. Mavis, who arrived fully developed at twelve, shared a room with Triggy, Ann and Liz briefly, until Ann and Triggy left, and then slept by herself in the smallest room on the girls' floor when Liz moved in with just Janet, Caroline and I.

There were many departures too, in those years; those friends of my little girlhood, some of whom I would not see again for many years. Leslie, Terry Mac, Peter, Gerry and Pauline all joined my sister at Rutland Gate until it closed in the summer of 1954. Peter, Terry Mac and Gerry came down to Silverlands most weekends. Most of the boys did a stint in National Service: Terry Mac and Charlie enlisted the Air Force and Peter went into the Army, where he saw action in Cyprus. Eddie joined the Merchant Navy for a few years, and then immigrated to Canada and, eventually, worked as producer for the Canadian Broadcasting Company.

Ann left at sixteen, became a secretary, married twice, and moved to Sydney, Australia where she still lives with her second husband Bob. Forty-five years later, she came back into my life with vivid memories of our childhood. Hers were much more vivid than mine, since she was five years older.

Brian had left Stepgates for good when he turned fifteen in 1952. His mother did not want him and never had, and there was no future for him in London. Mr. Waddington and the Committee decided that he could work as handy man and gardener under Bert Hazell. For the first few months, he continued to live at Silverlands and worked with Mr. Hazell for about forty-four hours a week. For this, he was paid a measly two shillings and sixpence. Later, Brian was invited to live with Mr. and Mrs. Hazell; their sons, Eric and Brian, were his age. Permission was given and Brian went to stay with them, earning the grand sum of one pound, six shillings a week from which he proudly paid for his room and board.

Sometime in 1954, Brian became very ill and he had to be hospitalized at Saint Peter's. The doctors said he needed an emergency operation. His mother would not give permission (our parents were always consulted about medical matters), so the Committee, at Mr. Waddington's urging, gave the go-ahead for the surgery and Brian got well again. But he grew tired of working so hard and not being one of us anymore. He loved the Hazells, but he wanted to return to Guernsey. On New Year's Eve 1954, Brian disappeared and on New Year's Day 1955, he turned up in Guernsey, and that was the last time any of us children saw or heard from him for more than forty years. However, he always kept in touch with the Hazell family.

Brian sent me a copy of Patrick Waddington's letter, sent to him in Guernsey after he ran away. It was written on the official Actors Orphanage stationary, with all the famous actor/producer Committee members listed down the left-hand side (Noël Coward, still President). More than any words I could write, this letter demonstrates Patrick Waddington's care and concern for us.

My Dear Brian,

Firstly I have to thank you very much for the charming gift you made me at Christmastime, it was much appreciated. Now, my dear boy, I have to add that it was very unkind of you, having made up your mind to travel home to Guernsey, not to have sent some message to Mrs. Hazell the moment you arrived safely.

Poor Mrs. Hazell, who has been a wonderful foster-mother to you, was most distressed and anxious; so indeed was I. You need not have felt that you had to escape by such secretive methods.

If you can remember, almost exactly a year ago, I offered to pay for you to go home to Guernsey, if you decided that was your ambition, despite your mother's refusal to have anything to do with you. If you had come to me and just told me that you wished to go, everything could have been arranged tidily, and I would not have allowed anything to prevent you going.

Now I am both relieved and delighted to hear that you are with friendly kind people in Guernsey, and I hope you will be happy and contented, and work hard for your new employers. By separate package I am dispatching your Post Office Savings Book, together with your National Insurance Card, a case with most of your clothes in it, which Mrs. Hazell has carefully packed and an additional parcel with further belongings.

Please, now sit down and write a kind letter to Mrs. Hazell, she is very fond of you, and I know it would please her to hear from you. I too, should like to get a postcard from you every now and then, just to know you are all right.

With every sort of good wish to you for 1955.
Patrick W. S. Waddington

Brian eventually married Helen and had two daughters. For the first few years, he worked as a stevedore in St. Peter Port. Later, for many years, he was a successful Guernsey artist with his own gallery, winning many awards. When Brian died in May 2009, his coffin was painted by his artist friends with scenes of Guernsey and, before the funeral, it was taken for a drive to all his favorite places on the island.

In 1953, two new housemasters arrived to replace Gordon: Alasdair Fraser, the handsome Scot and Mr. Hayward, yet another ex-military man, who had been a Wing Commander in the Air Force. They introduced us to hobbies in the old classrooms, off the outer courtyard. We had painting, botany and wild-flower collecting, woodworking, sewing and piano lessons and it was there that Brian discovered his latent talent as an artist. Chris became an ardent botanist, he had a room in the basement where he studied his specimens and, after he left Silverlands, he continued his passion for nature, working at a field study centre on the border of England and Wales.

A few of us took piano lessons. I learned the notes and how to read music, but I had neither the gift nor the staying power. However, Gerry did teach us all to play *Chopsticks*.

Gerry had succeeded Ken as head boy, when Ken left for Rutland Gate. On Sunday afternoons, as we all listened to *Family Favourites* on the radio and sang along to *Sipping Soda through a Straw* and *If You Drop a Silver Dollar on the Ground*, Gerry, doing a sort of early karaoke, would imitate Mario Lanza singing *Because,* earning his nickname *Geraldo Normini*. Dark haired and very good-looking, he was a kind and generous boy who was to become an equally kind and caring man. Gerry had come to Silverlands in 1949 after his actor father died tragically in a freak stage accident. (In 1947, Harold Norman, playing the title role in *Macbeth*, was stabbed for real during the final sword fight and later died of his wounds. His ghost is now said to haunt the Coliseum Theatre in Oldham, where the fatal scene was played. Harold Norman's death is often cited as one of the reasons why actors are superstitious about *Macbeth* and consider it a bad luck play.)

Gerry moved on to Rutland Gate for the year before it closed, but he always came down on weekends. He had a job with British Airways, but his heart was always in the performing arts and he often dabbled in nightclub acts. He must have been thrilled to be cast, by Richard Attenborough, in a small role in Gandhi. *Gerry died of a heart attack just a few weeks before our first reunion in 2000, an event he, almost more than anyone, would have loved.*

The truly gifted musician among us was Janet. Whenever I hear *The Moonlight Sonata* on the radio, I always think of Janet for she practiced it for hours on the grand piano in the Assembly room. She had a good ear and could play a mean *Boogie Woogie* and almost any popular song on request. Janet and her twin, Bernie, had come to Silverlands after their father died in 1951. They were nine when they arrived, a year older than I was. Janet and I were in the same dormitory for a few years. Janet left school and Silverlands when she was sixteen in 1958. Bernie stayed on, a little while longer, until Silverlands closed.

Bernard went into the police force and later worked in business. He died in 2005 leaving three children. Janet was to die of cancer at only twenty-eight. When she became ill, Kirsten and David Slater took her into their home and, after she died, her little daughter Heidi was brought up as a member of the Slaters' growing family.

During Mr. Waddington's tenure, au pair girls from several different countries started coming to work at Silverlands, each for a short stay: Marianne, she of the bare-breasted handstands on the beach, and Lena from Germany. Later on, Birgitte and Juta came from Denmark. They helped the staff with various tasks and were a breath of fresh air. The girls liked them for their different clothes and their lilting accented English. The older boys and younger masters liked them for different reasons!

In 1953, one of the former old boys, Tony Holmes, came back to work as an under housemaster, but he stayed for only three months. Tony and his brother Tim had both been at Langley Hall and were at Silverlands when I first arrived. Tony would have been twenty-one when he returned as a junior staff member. He was the son of Sir Henry Ainley, the film and West End stage star. (The Actors' Orphanage was sometimes a convenient place for the unwanted offspring of famous actors; those born on 'the wrong side of the sheets').

Tony studied at RADA and, after his father died, Tony took the name Anthony Ainley and went on to gain fame as an actor in his own right: in the long running television series Upstairs Downstairs *and as The Master in the even longer running series,* Doctor Who. *After he became famous, he wanted nothing to do with any of us! His brother Tim still lives on Long Island in the States.*

Mr. Hayward was asked to leave after only a short while with us, and was replaced by Mr. Duvall, who I liked him very much and was sad to see him leave the following year. Housemasters, like earlier matrons, came for a short time and left for reasons unknown to us. Obviously someone with staying power, Alasdair Fraser was appointed headmaster and Mr. Waddington found it safe to spend his time at the office in London now that we were in two pairs of good Scottish hands: Mr. Fraser and dear Miss Rennie, who having arrived as Matron at the end of Miss Berry's reign of terror, stayed on to see me through puberty.

TWELVE

Growing Things and Other Developments

WHEN I WAS ten, our mother decided to change our names from our father's surname, Moore, to her maiden name, White. Susannah, then fourteen, announced that it made us sound like bastards. Mother replied she would rather have us seem to be bastards than be known as *his* children. For years, Sue and I wondered what it was that our father had done that made Mother so vindictive. She would never talk about him, even after he came back into Susannah's life and we were grown women.

> *It wasn't until Mother died in 1999 that we learned from Gina about Mother having placed a restraining order on Father. The order said that he could have nothing to do with us until we were twenty-one.*
>
> *After Mother's memorial service, Sue said to me, "Do you want to go and find out more about our father? I know Gina is still alive. She's living in Putney with her sister Tessa." Of course, I said, "Yes." And so, off we went to Putney the next day. Gina, the widow of Father's boyhood friend, Ted Ware, was also the youngest sister of Aunty Monica, Father's sister-in-law, who had invited us to stay in Wimbledon for those few weekends long ago.*

Father's younger brother Arthur was married to Aunty Monica and they lived at 37 Home Park Road in Wimbledon, just across from the Wimbledon Common and those world-famous tennis courts. Until Sue went to Canada, she and I spent a few weekends with Uncle Arthur and Aunty Monica, with both Mother's and Audrey's grudging permission.

I was to learn much later on, when I was living in America that Uncle Arthur had stayed in touch with us at Father's request; keeping him informed about how we were and where we were. Whether Arthur did it willingly, I have my doubts, but I'm sure Aunty Monica did.

Uncle Arthur was rather stout with a square and florid face. He wore his thinning hair with, what would be called today, a 'comb-over.' He always dressed in immaculately ironed white shirts, knife-edge-creased pants and a cardigan sweater and, while he was never unpleasant, there was something creepy about him. As we were leaving, he would press a large, white five-pound note into each of our hands. I never felt comfortable around him. Once, I got up the nerve to ask him if he knew where my father was. He gave me a steely look and harshly told me I was never to mention Father again. *Knowing what Gina told us later, I am now sure those five pound notes came from Father.*

Auntie Monica was dark and pretty. The eldest of five sisters whose father had been a wine chandler from Genoa, Monica and her sisters had all been born in Turin. The family had immigrated to Cardiff when Gina, the youngest, was a baby. Aunty Monica always told us, when we asked why she collected all those Flamenco dolls and framed bull-fight posters, that she was descended from the sailors from the Spanish Armada who had washed up on the shores of Wales. At ten or eleven, I believed her. We never ever knew they were Italian, but I suspect they kept that quiet because Italy had sided with Germany in World War II. *Oh, the things they kept quiet about in our family!*

Aunty Monica always wore a thick layer of pancake make-up, had her black hair in a big bun at the nape of her neck and wore frilly, long sleeved blouses, buttoned up to her neck and down to her wrist.

> *Gina told us the reason for this covering up, she said, "That Arthur beat my poor sister black and blue, and she, silly cow, wouldn't leave him. She'd say to me, 'Who will fix my pappy's dinner and iron his clothes?'" But we never knew that then.*

Their home seemed the height of luxury to us, whenever we went to visit these seemingly wealthy, childless relatives of our missing father. The house was brick with a small front garden, a bow window, a chiming front door bell and a Pianola – a player piano, with lots of piano rolls: 'KKKKaty,' 'Jealousy' 'Lady of Spain' and more. You just pedaled away and pretended you were actually playing. Uncle Arthur's pride and joy was the barbecue grill on the stone terrace in front of the immaculately mowed back lawn. Uncle Arthur had earned this middle class splendor as a very successful turf accountant. He was a bookie!

Back to that September day after Mother died. Sue and I took Gina and Tessa for a pub lunch at The Angel, just down the road from their tiny ground floor flat. Then we all walked back slowly, Tessa dragging her oxygen tank, to their flat and their rather pokey, smoky sitting room. As Sue and I sat down gingerly on their ancient, over sprung sofa, Gina, lighting up a cigarette, said,

"So, did you girls know that your dad was gay?"

We said, yes we did. Sue had seen quite a lot of father towards the end of his life. She had returned to England from Canada with her husband and small son after receiving his telegram that said, 'I can see you now that you are twenty-one.' He was living with a younger man at that time. Sue wrote to me about him. I was eighteen and living in New York.

I never did meet my father.

Gina told us that, in her opinion, the charges about Father finagling his imprest funds during the war were trumped up. She said Father had always kept in touch with her and her late husband, Ted, and what happened according to Father was this. He had made a pass at an officer, whom he thought was of similar persuasion. His instinct was wrong. He was reported and charges were brought against him. (Until the Wolfendon Act was passed in 1966, just being a homosexual was a crime in England punishable by imprisonment.) Could he have faced a court-martial for simply making a pass, especially, since he had been doing such a highly commended job in public relations for the Western Command? It would have been difficult, if not impossible, to prove. So when they discovered he had altered one or two invoices, albeit for a few shillings and pence, to cover out of pocket expenses he had incurred in the line of duty, the homophobes had their case.

According to Gina, Father had been happy and doing well in his job until May of 1942, when his superior officer was promoted and a new man took over. Shortly after, this new superior officer reported him to the higher ups, and he was given notice terminating his services under his contract on June 11, 1942. However, someone had commenced court martial proceedings before he could simply be terminated. If the court martial proceedings hadn't already started, he would simply have been sacked.

Gina insisted that our mother knew the truth of the matter, and therefore it could not have been because she thought he was an embezzler that she kept him away from us. Gina suspected it was the negative publicity, engendered by Father being cashiered, that had damaged Mother's pride. Therefore, she blamed him for her inability to get future starring roles. Also, she didn't even request the restraining order until the war was over and Father had left our home for good. And, because all this happened after her long run in Junior Miss in 1943 and 1944 was over, (the last 'child' role she was to play), the lack of good roles could be put down to the fact that she was simply getting too old to play teenagers.

When I consider now that all three men Mother married were gay, I don't think Father's homosexuality was ever an issue, as far as we were concerned.

At eleven, burdened with my new surname, which I found hard to explain, I was relieved that I only had one more term at Frithwald and would be entering my new school, Sir William Perkins, with a surname that would hopefully stay the same for the rest of my school days.

I had developed a severe under-bite, which made me look rather truculent. After much discussion between the staff, the Committee and Mother, it was decided to send me to Great Ormond Street Hospital in London to have my incipient lower wisdom teeth removed. Those teeth had not yet burst through my gums and were just lying there: teeth-in-waiting. The surgeons proposed that when they removed those teeth, my jaw would spring back and I would, magically, lose the Neanderthal look.

So, up to Great Ormond Street I went and there, in the process of excavating with scalpels and pliers, they managed to also split the left side of my small mouth. This only added to my discomfort and truculence. I was given an aspirin for pain and, with a straw, I sipped Robinson's Barley Water for nutrients until I could eat again. I stayed at Rutland Gate for a couple of days following the surgery and I was fitted with a nasty pink plastic and wire retainer which would, incrementally, push my upper teeth forward and hopefully improve my looks. I loathed that retainer and, once home again in Chertsey, I flushed it down the toilet. Miss Rennie had my pocket money stopped until a new one was paid for.

Miss Rennie, as Matron, had the necessary nursing skills to be able to ascertain if we really were sick or faking it in order to miss school. When any of us did come down with a communicable disease, we were confined to the sick room. If there was anything around worth catching, we all tried to catch it. At various times, we had measles both regular and German, whooping cough, mumps, strep throat, tonsillitis, and various strains of influenza. Everyone, except for me, had the chicken pox, although I made myself constantly available.

I never did catch it, even years later when my daughters had it.

When we caught the regular measles, Liz, Janet, Caroline, Ann, Pauline and I convalesced in the big dormitory. We had to keep the curtains drawn and we weren't allowed to read because we might damage our eyes. One morning, the same old lumpy porridge was sent up for our breakfast. In a spirit of defiance, and with no one to stand over us and make us eat it, we tossed our porridge up on top of the wardrobe. Today, somewhere out there is a large oak wardrobe with a pile of petrified porridge stuck to the top.

I came down with a bad case of flu when I was ten. Alone in the sick room, I was feeling sorry for myself when Richard Attenborough came in. He sat down on the end of my bed, chatted with me and read me a story. I didn't know then he was famous; he was just a nice man, a member of the Committee. He and his pretty blonde wife, Sheila Sim, lived nearby in Richmond and they often came down to visit us. "Popping in," he called it. "Just to see how you are all doing." He was short and very boyish looking, then.

When *The Baby and the Battleship* came to the Chertsey Playhouse, we all went to see it and were loudly proud in front of the local kids, because *we actually knew him.* Those were times when it paid to be an actor's child. It didn't pay that well too often, but saying you knew Richard Attenborough was *always* good for you.

Noël Coward continued to come down from time to time in his capacity as President, but every time he came, the press got wind of it and his visits became photo opportunities. While these were good for making the public aware of us for fundraising purposes, his visits were never very informal. When Attenborough came to Silverlands, he came as an interested friend, not as a famous personality with a photographer in tow. Ray wrote,

> Of all the things I remember, one day stands out. A young
> Richard Attenborough and his lovely wife took me and a friend
> to Regents Park Zoo, for a day's outing. Before returning to
> Silverlands we visited the Attenborough's house in Richmond.
> I felt, that day, like part of a family, as we had so much fun.
> That's what I imagined families did. Every time I see Lord
> Attenborough in a film, I recall that day when I was nine."

Liz and Caroline stayed at the Attenborough's house on the night before Queen Elizabeth II's coronation, 2 June 1953. Five kids were chosen to watch the royal parade, which was to pass near the Attenborough's house. Liz, Caroline, Gerry (then head boy), Carl and Charlie all slept on the floor of the spare room. None of them ever forgot the uniformed maid who served them breakfast in the morning before they left for the parade.

The rest of us got to watch the Coronation in the Assembly Room on the wonderful new projection television set – a gift from Noël Coward. From a wooden box on casters, the picture was projected onto a large screen against the wall. Not understanding how it worked, small boys would stand between the box and the screen, gaping at the moving picture and be told to 'Move it' by the rest of us as we watched the golden coach go by (in black and white). Later, I remember watching *The Four Feathers* with John Clements and Ralph Richardson and my favorite American Western, *Champion the Wonder Horse*.

Years later, in 1981, I had occasion to write to Richard Attenborough about Shakespeare & Company, the American theatre company where I was director of public relations. He wrote to me on his return from

India after filming Gandhi *saying,*

"I was delighted to hear from you and hear your news. Naturally, if the company does come to England, I should be more than happy to do anything I can to help, and in any event would be thrilled to see you. Again, thank you for writing. I too sign this, love! Richard."

The company never did go to England and so nothing came of it, but, in the past, I always felt that I could call and he'd be there. At that time, he was Chairman of the Board of Capital Radio, which had purchased the ailing and run-down Duke of York's Theatre. Capital Radio had restored the theatre to its pre-World War II glory,(the way it had looked when my father had been the manager and where my parents had met and married). Enclosed with the above letter, Richard Attenborough sent me the souvenir program of the Gala re-opening (in aid of the Combined Theatrical Charities, of which the Orphanage was one). My father is mentioned in it, and he thought I would like to have some remembrance of him.

Just as when at Langley Hall sweeping changes had occurred in 1934 when Noël Coward took over, so did much needed changes begin around 1953 when, at Coward's encouraging, Richard Attenborough became actively involved – but he would not take on the Presidency – he felt it needed a bigger name. So, when Coward left England for Jamaica in 1956 after twenty-two years as President, he was succeeded by Laurence Olivier, who rarely visited Silverlands. Attenborough became very involved as Chairman.

In 1993, Queen Elizabeth II created Richard Attenborough, Baron of Richmond Hill. He had served as Chairman of the Actors' Orphanage Fund, later The Actors' Charitable Trust, from 1956 until 1989 when Lord Olivier died. He then became President and later President Emeritus. He and Lady Attenborough have been tireless in their work on behalf of the elderly members of the profession at Denville Hall, as well as continuing to care about the less fortunate children and their families. Like Coward, he was a very active Committee member, interested and involved in the day-to-day happenings of our lives.

Once a month, some members of the Committee – Edith Evans, Nicholas Hannen, Jessie Winter, Lorn Lorraine or Jill Esmond – would come and chat with us, to see how we were doing. They seemed to come more frequently, then. Perhaps it was through a continuing concern that Gordon had traumatized us and they wanted to ensure *that* was over?

Most of us were fairly resilient children and our new headmaster, Alasdair Fraser, was a stern yet kind man. The scars of Gordon remained, and for some of us never quite went away, but we were glad he was gone and these new, kinder people had come.

Mr. Fraser, who had been hired as "Housemaster and Agricultural Advisor," started a Young Farmers Club and farming of a sort began. He valiantly tried to get us interested in the land, and indeed it did rub off on some of us: Chris became a professional gardener and naturalist, and Ray, in far off Tasmania, and Liz and I, in America, are avid gardeners. Others are as well, I'm sure.

The field just adjacent to the cricket pitch and football field was ploughed under and planted with seed potatoes. All spring and summer long, we hoed and, in August, we harvested. On Saturday mornings, all of us, big and small, filled dozens of burlap sacks with those spuds, which the big boys then hefted into wheel barrows and took up to the house to be stored for our future meals. The girls had kitchen duty, helping the cooks prepare meals for fifty people. Usually our chores were washing, peeling, gouging out the eyes and cutting up just enough of those potatoes, say a hundred or so, for the cooks to boil for supper. We also cleaned and prepared the other vegetables or washed eggs and candled them, too. Mr. Hazell had been asked to expand the kitchen garden and we were encouraged to help in it. We weeded, hoed and picked beans, carrots, turnips, Swedes, parsnips, marrows and cabbages. We gathered apples and plums from the fruit trees and picked gooseberries, blackberries and currants.

And then there were the chickens: at least thirty of them came to live, and die, on the hillside by the back drive. A large enclosure was built with two chicken coops. For two years, we scraped chicken poop off the rafters and roosts and collected the eggs. The big boys' job was to kill the chickens for supper. With an ax and a chopping block the boys cut of their heads and those silly headless chickens would run around until, realizing what little brains they had were gone, they finally fell down. All of this activity was part the Young Farmer's Club. Ann, being the oldest girl, was put in charge of the Club's money. When she mislaid it, Mr. Fraser made her pay it back out of her pocket money. It took her eight weeks, she said.

Beatings were now a thing of the past, except for some moderate slippering of the especially naughty little boys, but we still had punishments. Caught swearing one day, Mr. Fraser took me down to one of the smallest basement rooms. Six dead chickens were hanging by their feet.

"There now, lassie," he said, "you are to pluck every single feather from these birds, including all the little pinfeathers. While you are doing this, I want you to think about why you should not use swear words."

It took me forever to pluck those chickens. I still do swear occasionally. I can't help it. I was learning how to swear from the age of four.

By far the worst punishment from Mr. Fraser was the dreadful day that Liz was expelled. We were all ordered to go directly to the Assembly Room after breakfast. We were chattering away thinking we were going to have a treat: a trip to the theatre or something. Mr. Fraser came in looking grim. We all sat down. He cleared his throat and said,

"Elizabeth is to be expelled for one year."

Liz was in such a shock she nearly fell off her seat. She just sat there, speechless. She remembers being told to get her few things together – we never had much in the way of belongings, never owned very much in all the years we were there.

That very day, Liz was shipped out. I remember crying. Everyone was upset. A tactless staff member told Caroline that she would never see her sister again and Caroline became so hysterical, they sent her upstairs and made her stay in her room for the rest of the day. She sat on her bed, staring out of the window, watching for Liz.

Their stepmother, Jane, went straight down to Silverlands when she was told that Liz was to be expelled. Jane said she couldn't imagine why they would expel such a sweet child. Mr. Fraser took Jane into the office where all the staff were seated and said to her, "Either Elizabeth goes or the entire staff go." Guess who went!

The Silverlands car took Liz to the home of the Reverend and Mrs. Archibald. He was Vicar of St. Peter's Church in Chertsey. All the time Liz was there, Mrs. Archibald was apparently very ill. Liz had to help in the house and do chores, "Just like I was their servant!" She said. She was expected to attend every church service, so she used to sit in the back of the church and, when the Vicar wasn't looking, she would slip out and walk around Chertsey. The Archibald family had a pet rabbit and Vicar Archibald made her go out every night down Church Lane, a narrow alley alongside the church, and pick dandelion leaves for that rabbit.

Liz told me,

> Oh, how I wanted to make that darn rabbit into a pie. That rabbit was so fat. I would stay out for hours and Vicar Archibald would get mad, but he still made me go out every night and roam the streets of Chertsey looking for dandelions for that stupid rabbit.

To this day, Liz has no idea why she was sent to the Archibalds. None of us knew either why Liz was expelled or that she was only a mile away from us all *for one whole year!* She thinks she was expelled for locking Mr. Fraser and one of the au pair girls, the buxom Marianne, in the linen closet, but I think there were probably other reasons, too. The staff at that time could be rather quixotic.

After Liz came back, none the worse for it really, she and I were grounded for climbing out of our bedroom window to see James Dean in *Rebel without a Cause* at the Chertsey Playhouse, without permission. I was climbing up the ivy to our bedroom and saw Mr. Fraser sitting on the end of Liz's bed. I almost fell on Liz who was underneath me. Considering Liz's recent expulsion, Fraser just seemed rather amused at our escapade and grounded us for only a week. Like I said, quixotic.

When all the staff had to go up to London for a big meeting, Mr. Fraser put Ann and Gerry in charge. Everyone ran wild. He never put any one of us in charge again. A lot of the new arrivals like Gay, Sarah, Mavis and James, didn't like Fraser and thought he was mean, but they hadn't known Gordon. Fraser was our knight in shining armour compared to Gordon. Ann used to ride her bike to Lyne shop and buy cigarettes for him.

One summer, he took Liz and Caroline up to Scotland for a holiday to stay with his parents. His father was a minister in the Church of Scotland. Liz said his mother gave them lovely scented baths with Pears Soap. She thinks that perhaps she was asked to Scotland to make amends for her being expelled, but perhaps it was because she and Caroline have Scottish blood.

I actually did like Mr. Fraser, even though he had made me pluck those bloody chickens. He was basically a fair man and up until now my experience of many adults had not found them very fair. Well, maybe the Savage-Baileys, but I was getting older and beginning to think things through. Up until now, I had accepted the way things were at Silverlands; I kept my head down as much as possible and rolled with the punches. I guess I blocked things out. But Gordon had changed that. Now, I started to show some emotion.

In the winter of 1953-54, I had taken the 11 Plus exam and passed, the first Orphanage girl to do so. Chris and Terry had passed it earlier and gone to Woking Grammar School for Boys, Now I would be going to a Grammar School for Girls. Feeling rather pleased and proud, I asked permission to use the pay phone, under the front hall stairs, to call my mother. Permission granted, I dialed PADdington 9324, her house in London. At the sound of ringing, I put tuppence in the slot and pressed button A. I remember the conversation as if it were yesterday.

I said, "Hullo Mummy, it's Judy. I have something to tell you."

"Have you, darling. Is everything all right?"

"Yes, everything is wonderful. I just found out that I've passed the 11 Plus exam."

"How lovely for you, darling," and then she said, "I have some good news, too. Uncle Tony Guthrie is arranging for me to live in Canada next year, and Sue will come over and join me when she finishes school…" and on she went, full of *her* news.

By now my heart had sunk to my stomach and I was close to tears. The pips came.

I said, "I have to go now, Mummy, I have no more change. Good bye."

I hung up the phone, stood there in that little cupboard under the stairs in the dark and cried.

THIRTEEN

A Merit Based Education

IN THE SPRING of 1954, having passed the 11 Plus exam and before I was finally enrolled at Sir William Perkins School for Girls in Chertsey, my mother, who was busily involved in selling her house at 16 Linhope Street and preparing to immigrate to Canada, decided that I must be bright and therefore she should step in, with one of her grand maternal flourishes, and see if I, her younger daughter, shouldn't perhaps go to a school with more prestige, – providing, of course, I could get a full scholarship.

She made the appropriate enquiries, pulled strings and it was arranged that I should go up to London for an interview at the venerable and prestigious St. Paul's School for Girls, with its sterling reputation for educating young women. That spring, Mother was appearing in Dodie Smith's *I Capture the Castle* at the Aldwych Theatre in the West End, which was to be her last West End appearance for many years. Dodie Smith was a St. Paul's old girl and had arranged an introduction.

On a rainy spring day, I was put on the train to Waterloo, met by Mother clad in her furs, a jaunty little hat and a little too much perfume and taken by taxi to St. Paul's in Hammersmith. I remember very little of that day. I didn't want to go. I hated London, it was noisy, dirty, tree-less and I didn't know anyone. What I do remember is that St. Paul's School was old, cold and grey. It was filled with large girls with frightfully posh accents and hyphenated names and the headmistress, or High Mistress as she was called, Miss Osborn, was most forbidding. I spoke very little, mumbled, "I don't know" to most questions and, to my mother's chagrin, flunked the interview and any chance of a scholarship.

I was relieved. I didn't want to leave my Silverlands family and the Surrey countryside where I had grown up. It was bad enough that, when

I was properly enrolled at Sir William Perkins, I would have to walk to school alone, without any of my fellow orphans, for the first time in my life, and because of *that* I was filled with fear and trepidation. I would have to walk or bicycle the mile and a half to Pycroft, the junior school, along the same route we had all walked *together* to Frithwald for years, only no-one would walk with me. All the other children would be going by van or bus to other secondary modern and primary schools in the area.

I would have to sit in a classroom with girls who came from *normal* homes. Girls with a mother, who stayed at home, and a father, who had a regular day job. Girls who had brothers and sisters, each with their own bedrooms, who wore new clothes bought especially for them at Marks & Spencer and who went on trips in the family car and, oh God it was going to be awful! I just knew it. Also, my uniform would be different from those worn by the other kids at Silverlands. I'd be different; different at Silverlands *and* different at Perkins. I did not want to be different.

Before school started, Mr. Waddington took me to Woking, to the shop that, exclusively, sold William Perkins uniforms. I had to have a navy blue tunic; a navy blue hat with a yellow and navy ribbon; navy blue gym shorts; navy blue knee socks; new navy blue knickers and a navy blue blazer. And I had to have a white shirt, not a blouse, a shirt, as well as a white Aertex gym shirt and a white liberty bodice (to wear under the shirts). Later on, I would get a white cotton bra, but not yet. Around my neck, I would wear the school tie, navy with yellow and white diagonal stripes, and on my feet, brown or black lace-up shoes.

Why it was Mr. Waddington who took me school shopping I do not know? I suspect he loved to shop and fancied himself quite an arbiter of taste. More importantly, he held the Orphanage's meagre purse strings? We drove into Woking and entered the fine old shop with wooden paneling and sweet elderly sales ladies. In the rear of the shop a complete Perkins' uniform was brought for me to try on in the changing room. I had never been in a changing room before. I put everything on with the sales lady's help, and came out to show Mr. Waddington my finery. My blazer was very smart; it had the ornate school crest embroidered in yellow, white and gold on the top pocket with the Latin motto *A spe in spem* under the shield. Mr. Waddington said it meant "From hope to hope." I was some hope?

The sales lady had a good eye and everything fit me perfectly.

Mr. Waddington smiled and said, "Very nice, m'dear"

To the sales lady he said, "Do you have a longer tunic? Also, a slightly, larger blazer perhaps? They are rather dear and we have to make this uniform last, don't we, Judy?"

The sales lady obliged and returned with a tunic to fit a much taller person than chubby little me. I tried it on. The tunic came almost to my ankles. Regulation school length stipulated, 'The hem of the tunic should fall just below the knee.'

"That's better." he said, "Matron can take up the hem."

The second blazer's gorilla length sleeves hung well below my hands, but it seemed that Matron could take those up, too. Fortunately, my solid little body filled out the upper part of these larger sizes quite well.

Our purchases were packed into large boxes with white tissue paper and Mr. Waddington and I carried them to the school estate wagon and drove back to Silverlands. There, later that day, Miss Rennie had me try everything on again and I stood on a chair, with many admonitions not to fidget, while she put pins around the tunic skirt and blazer sleeves.

For the next five years, I wore that tunic. At first, it had a rather fat hem. Each year, as I grew, the hem was let down and my tunic sported bands of varying shades of navy blue, for with each adjustment a new, less-faded shade was revealed. I wore the blazer for two or three years and was allowed a new one when my bust developed and I could no longer button it – Gay was to get my hand-me-down. At the beginning of summer term, no matter what the temperature, we wore yellow and blue checked dresses that looked, from a distance, like the color of fresh manure. Our winter hats resembled a sailor hat, circular and stiffened with whalebone, with a yellow and navy hatband. The hat was supposed to be worn flat on top of one's head. In the summer, we wore straw boaters with the school ribbons trailing down our backs.

It was against school rules to be seen in uniform without one's hat on, when not on the school grounds. Our winter hats were hated among the less correct students (and I quickly became one of them). It was common practice to try and immediately break down their stiffness by breaking up the whalebone. We would leave them out on hedges overnight or ride our bicycles over them. One girl even went so far as to lay hers on the railway track at Chertsey Station to let the trains run over it. The tamed hats were more bearable to wear and the good girls were easy to spot because, after a year, their hats were still stiff and looking like new. I had no problem breaking in my hat; the boys at Silverlands were a great help and did it for me.

On my first day, Mr. Fraser drove me to Pycroft the junior school – from then on I was allowed to ride my bicycle. The first two years of my grammar school education were spent in the intimacy of Pyrcroft, a lovely ivy-covered, old house in a walled garden, and a ten-minute walk from the upper school. Part of the house dated back to Elizabethan times. It was a friendly place for eleven and twelve year old girls with its small classrooms. The uneven floors and steep, crooked staircases must have been trying for the teachers. We were told that Charles Dickens had once been a guest at Pyrcroft and had the house in mind when he wrote *Oliver Twist*.

In Chapter XXII, Dickens describes how Bill Sikes and Toby Crackit take young Oliver with them to a house they planned to rob in Chertsey. They needed a small boy able to climb through a scullery window and open the door. Dickens wrote, *'After walking a quarter of a mile, they stopped before a detached house surrounded by a wall, to the top of which Toby Crackit, scarcely pausing to take a breath, climbed in a twinkling.'* And then later, describing the small entry, *'It was a little lattice window, about five feet and a half above the ground, at the back of the house, which belonged to a scullery, or some brewing place, at the end of the passage.'* There *was* a little barred window, just like that, at the bottom of the main staircase. For English Literature, that first year, we read *Oliver Twist* and the story came alive for us knowing that a tiny part of it took place where we were.

Classes were held in the former parlor, the sitting room, the dining room, and in two of the upstairs bedrooms; five classes with no more than fourteen girls in each. I was in 3M for my first year and Lower 4P, my second, before I moved up to Upper 4L in the main school on the Guildford Road. The 'L' meant you would continue to take Latin. All of us took Latin at Pyrcroft. There were just eleven of us in 3M that first year, so our classes were held in the smallest bedroom upstairs; our desks all huddled together in no particular order.

In the early 1950s, before the mania for celebrities took over, being the child of an actress was tantamount to being the child of a loose woman. In my first year, some girls, and many mistresses I was sure, looked askance at me for the error of my birth, the hopelessness of my clothes, my battered bicycle and my handed down satchel. In my initial misery, I got comfort from '*Cookie,*' the Pyrcroft cook. A kind woman, she said to me, one day when I was feeling down and left out,

> Keep your chin up, girl. They're no better than you are.
> Birth has nothing to do with a person's mettle. You
> got in here, didn't you, in spite of all the strikes against
> you? Don't let them see it hurts. Children are cruel and
> they'll only be crueler if they see you are hurting.

I took her good advice and learned to use my wits. Growing up with more 'brothers' than anyone at Perkins, I knew a great deal about 'the birds and the bees,' certainly more than most of my schoolmates. I fed them tidbits, a little at a time, parceling out my information. In seeking acceptance that first year, I became the 'go-to' girl with that certain kind of knowledge and, later, I became the class clown.

In my first year, Mrs. Showell taught Arithmetic and Religious Instruction. A large, gentle woman, she and her husband had been missionaries in China. She told us lots of colourful stories about China. The one I best remember was how, after Mao Tse-tung's communists had gained power in 1949, all the Chinese ladies with bound feet were ordered to remove their 'bandages of vanity.' When they did, Mrs. Showell told us, their toes fell off. We were eleven and rather ghoulish, so we loved those stories.

It was because we were eleven and ghoulish, and Mrs. Showell was so inordinately kind and patient, that she was considered fair game, especially during Religious Instruction. We surreptitiously passed around slips of paper with book, chapter and verse references to *Lot lay with his daughters,* and other choice sentences. Or, with our Bibles in front of us,

I, anxious to win friends, would ask innocently, "Mrs. Showell, if you please, what is circumcision?"

Poor Mrs. Showell, anxious to educate, would harrumph a bit and say, "Well – erum – it was a religious practice of removing the foreskin from the male children. Not for you girls to worry about. Ha, ha." Then, someone else would ask, "What is a foreskin?"

By the end of my first year, I finally felt accepted. But it was a tough year and, to this day, I feel some of those girls never truly accepted me. That first year at Perkins, I learned first hand about prejudice and what it can do to the soul.

One of my more painful school experiences had occurred in English class in the Lower Fourth at Pyrcroft. We were studying the Civil War in History – the Roundheads and Cavaliers – and our English teacher, attempting a little parallel learning, showed us a picture of William Yeames' painting of a Roundhead soldier asking the small son of a Cavalier, *"And When Did You Last See Your Father?"* Our classroom assignment was to write a paragraph answering that question from our more mundane personal lives. What could I say? Too intimidated to protest and lacking any information at all about my father, I couldn't and didn't do it. I got an F – an F for my Father.

If there was any one theme which ran through my years at Perkins it would have to be 'disorganized and untidy.' My report cards are filled with comments like, 'She could be more organized' or 'Her handwriting is untidy' or 'She should put her thoughts in order.' At Assembly, once I had moved up to the main school, many times our terrifying headmistress, Miss Margaret Sames, MA Oxon, would finish the morning prayers and her general remarks with:

"Judith White, your hair is a mess." (She always called me Judith, never acknowledging that my name was Judy).

"Judith White, detention for not wearing your hat with your school uniform." "Judith White, see me in my office directly."

I would stand anxiously outside her office, for what seemed hours, and when told to enter, I did so with my eyes downcast. She would then say something like,

"Judith, did I see you riding a cart horse this morning in your school uniform?"

"Yes, Miss Sames."

"Why, child?"

"Well you see, ma'am, I got a puncture and I had to leave my bicycle in the ditch. I didn't want to be late for school and when Mr. Jones our milkman came along – he has the farm near Silverlands – he offered me a ride."

"But child, you were riding astride the horse with your skirt up in a most unladylike fashion. I, myself, saw you dismount and your knickers were visible. Judith, I am going to have to give you a detention, and a note to take back to the Orphanage. I give you a lot of leeway knowing your home circumstances, but we at this school must insist that our girls behave like young ladies. Is that clear?"

"Yes, Miss Sames."

Suitably chastened, I went back to my classroom. But I never really did learn to be a lady.

Caught once standing on a table in the school library reciting *The Walrus and the Carpenter*, I was made to write out the entire poem twenty times, to remind me that libraries were for studying and silence. Writing 'lines' was a popular and not very creative form of punishment. To have to write a hundred times *"I will not talk in class,"* or *"I must wear my hat when in uniform,"* only served to make one's arm ache and one's index finger turn blue with ink. Copying *"The Walrus and the Carpenter"* twenty times at least served some purpose for I can still recite much of it to this day.

Once I settled into Perkins and became accepted by most of the girls, I maintained an average report card, never at the bottom or the top of the class. I did well in languages, English and history and poorly in science and arithmetic. In arithmetic, I flunked and flunked again and again. Some of us called our arithmetic teacher in the upper school as 'the one drip left in the drip-dry dress.' Nothing in her class ever inspired or encouraged me to learn arithmetic. She believed in rote learning and she never ever explained *why* we needed to understand how we arrived at our answers.

I did have two wonderfully inspiring teachers: Miss Littleboy, a six-foot tall Quaker lady, who made history live and breathe, and Miss Mount, who I can still see standing in front of Latin class, actively declining 'Ingens, Ingens,' her fists pumping the air with emphases. Under Miss Mount's guidance, the school put on a *Saturnalia* each year; our class acted out *Haec est Villa Iaccus* and later, *O Divina Clementina*. I got to play Clementina with large cardboard boxes (without topses) on my feet and without my spectacles, which guaranteed I would tumble off the stage during the performance, which I did much to everyone's delight.

For English literature, we put on the obligatory all-girls Shakespeare play each year. I was Snout in *A Midsummer Night's Dream* during my first year, and a rather short and pudgy Julius Caesar in a sheet in the Upper Fourth. I died very well, they said. Our English teacher was good and encouraged us to write with feeling. Having grown up learning to hide my feelings, I was always afraid of revealing too much of myself to others but once, I did get completely carried away. In the Lower Fifth, our assignment was to write an essay on a chapter we liked in *Wuthering Heights*. I filled page after page with purple prose about that last meeting between the two lovers, when Cathy lies dying. I had bodices heaving and Cathy and Heathcliff panting all over the place. I got a red A – was it a scarlet one – the school's highest mark.

At most outdoors games, I was athletically challenged. Consequently, I spent a great deal of time during physical education classes trudging or puffing around the cinder track. This track ran parallel to the railway line and all we puffing girls were always tooted at by the passing engineers and, a minute later, by the guards in the guards van. At netball, for me to get the ball into the net was nigh on impossible, in tennis getting the ball over the net was a challenge, and in the long-, high- and broad-jumps I was lucky if I reached the sand pit by falling face down. The only game I did passably well at was field hockey, perhaps because I had a stick to protect myself with. I played center half and, in spite of many painful whacks on the shins – my shin guards always slipping around the back of my legs – I enjoyed our games against visiting teams. As for any exertions in the gymnasium well, suffice it to say that the vaulting horse was not my friend, I never could touch my toes with ease and, if I had been a boy, the balance beam would have been my undoing – it nearly was in any case.

Our gym teacher got married during my last year. This made her quite a novelty and a curiosity. We never gave much thought to teachers having lives outside of school. That this particular teacher who was ancient – at least thirty – could have a 'boyfriend' was absolutely fascinating and the subject of much speculation.

Men rarely set foot on the school grounds. The school had a lady gardener and even the school cat was female. When some visiting male dignitary, a clergyman or the mayor of Chertsey, came to give out prizes and make a speech, the teachers fluttered around in their black robes like crows, making much of him.

This fawning over the opposite sex was something that I just couldn't understand. I had lived with thirty boys and masters since I was four. They weren't anything special. In fact, during all my teenage years, I never felt any particular yearning for the boys at Silverlands; they were like my brothers. I did get quite a crush on Charlie from Chertsey in my last year. I liked Charlie because he was nice to me and didn't ignore me or call me 'Four Eyes.' He was a kind young man and that's all it took for me to fall for him; but it never went anywhere, I doubt if he ever knew how I felt.

I was a late bloomer, but not so some of the others. Liz, Pauline and Gay both lusted after, and were lusted after in turn, by the boys at Silverlands and the boys from town, and my own sister was lusty from a very early age. Perhaps I was backward in the lust department, or maybe just shy. To me, boys were just that, boys. It was with ordinary social behavior that I struggled.

During my first year at Perkins, I sat next to Iris. She had short springy hair, a bouncy way of walking and she was friendly to me. For that I liked her – in spite of the fact that her hat was stiff. She invited me to come home with her one weekend. Miss Rennie gave me permission and I took my small belongings (toothbrush, flannel (washcloth), nightgown, and change of underwear in a brown paper bag) to school on the Friday.

I was very nervous. I was always ham-handed and wrong-footed, often as not, in the presence of strange adults. Iris's mother picked us up in her car. Their house was very nice, very clean and very small. Iris lived with just her mother and father and younger sister. They had a tiny front garden and a back garden with a lawn (not a field), flowerbeds and a small vegetable patch. It was all right out of an Enid Blyton novel. We went up the carpeted stairs and I was shown Iris's bedroom, where I was to sleep. It was all frilly and pink, with dainty little flowers on the wall-paper. The two beds had thick mattresses with two plump pillows each and pretty padded coverlets. Iris and her sister shared a bathroom with just one bathtub and one toilet, each pale yellow porcelain, not white, stained and chipped.

I unpacked my paper bag and we played a game of Ludo until her mother called us down to supper. The table, covered with a pure white cloth, had shining glasses and lovely *thin* china plates. Not being famil-iar with such niceties, I watched and learned. The food was delicious. I managed to eat nicely without dropping any food in my lap and I re-membered to say 'please' and 'thank you.' Iris' mother washed and ironed my clothes and cleaned my shoes after we had gone to bed that night.

The following day, we went to Windsor Castle and out for lunch. I tried to explain to Iris what Silverlands was like and realised that it was as foreign to her as her life was to me. Besides her father, she had rarely, if ever, talked to a person of the opposite sex. She had never climbed a tree, never used a swear word and never had to help with the housework or even clean her own shoes. She might as well have been from another planet. I was relieved when I was taken back to Silverlands in time for church on Sunday morning. I assumed that all my schoolmates lived like Iris. But they didn't. Iris and I grew apart after the first year and Hilary and Mary became my friends.

Visiting Hilary's rowdy, rough-and-tumble home several times during those school years, I saw that family life could be fun and re-laxing. Hilary lived with her Mum and Dad, her older sister, Valerie, and her two younger brothers, Andrew and Michael. Both boys were in wheelchairs, crippled with muscular dystrophy, but they were the most cheerful and comfortable family I knew when I was growing up. Hilary,

Mary and I remained friends through Perkins, losing touch for a while before we reconnected.

For my second year at Perkins, Gay joined me on the long walk or bike ride to school, and I was able to be the big sister and show her the ropes. Gay made a friend of a Chertsey girl, Jo, who lived with her Mum and Dad on Station Road. We used to go to Jo's house after school, where her Mum fussed over us 'poor wee girls', gave us tea and cakes, and let us watch television. On those days, we would often be late for high tea at Silverlands but we would say we had detention, which was believed because we so often did.

I still miss Gay in my life. She and I were close friends for a long, long while, well into our forties. She had arrived at Silverlands, with her young brother Bill, after their parents' rather acrimonious divorce. Her mother and mine had often tried out for the same roles during their long careers. Gay was as slender, pretty and delicate as I was not, and she seemed especially vulnerable to slights and name-calling. She and Bill arrived after Gordon left but, being unused to living with such a large number of people, she was cowed by it all.

In her adult life, when Gay was experiencing emotional and physical upheavals and so much unhappiness, she blamed much of her anguish on her few years at Silverlands and could not, would not, talk about it, even with me who had shared it with her. When I visited her at her husband's sheep farm in Wales in 1983, I had told her in detail about the horrors of Gordon and how, having known no other life, I was afraid I had become inured to it all and that I was possibly lacking an ability to feel. She replied that I was lucky to have had that ability beaten out of me. (It wasn't, I had just buried it deep.) But still, I loved her like a sister. Much later, on a second visit to Wales after her baby daughter was born prematurely and had died, I tried to enlist her mother-in-law's aid in getting some kind of emotional help for Gay. It didn't work. Gay called me, once I was back in America, accused me of meddling and we said some irretrievably awful things to each other. Because of that, I was unaware when she died at fifty-two of the wasting, possibly psychosomatic, illness that had plagued her last years. In response to my Christmas card, her husband wrote to me of her death. He said in his letter, 'Toward the end, life with her was very difficult, but when she was 'on' she was magic.' She was.

According to my Perkins's report book, which I have kept battered and torn in a bottom drawer in all the houses I have lived in, my scholastic record started with fairly high marks and went slowly downhill until I left in 1959. It never hit bottom, and I never failed a subject, but there was a steady decline in my marks, from As and Bs to Cs. On the graph of my educational life, the year my sister left for Canada my grades began to slide and never again rose to the highs of those first years at Pyrcroft. To those casually watching my progress, I passed muster but never lived up to my potential. Sir William Perkins was, in hindsight, a wonderful school and, while I wish I had paid more attention, I learned a great deal there; but there were inevitable pitfalls for one such as I.

FOURTEEN

Happy Families

In 2006, Susannah's friend, the late Patrick Newley, gave her a copy of our mother's entry in the 1955 British edition of Who's Who in Radio and Television. *He thought it would amuse us about her hobbies. After listing her birth, education etc, and past successes on stage, radio and television, the last sentence reads: 'No hobbies – has two children who take up all her time and interest.' Mother was on her way to Canada, leaving behind both those children, when this came out.*

Puberty finally arrived for me at thirteen. David and Kirsten Slater had been in residence for about eight months when I got my first period that winter Saturday afternoon. At that time, we used to go to a nearby estate and play squash on Saturdays. Why squash was chosen as our winter sporting activity, I have no idea, except perhaps that the facility was loaned to us and it was indoors, out of the weather. I was no better at squash than at any other games and after my time on the court, with that long racquet attempting to hit a very hard, fast and nasty little ball, I often ended up with many small round bruises on my body.

The day I got the curse, I left the court, battered and bowed as usual, and went into the girls' changing room. I pulled down my shorts and knickers, sat on the loo and let out a howl. There was a red sticky substance all over the inside of my thighs and the crotch of my navy blue knickers had a dark, stiffening patch.

"I'm bleeding," I sobbed, thinking I must have been hit too hard by the ball and had internal injuries. "I'm dying," I wailed. Liz, who was older than me, came into the cubicle with me.

"It's okay," she said, "you've just got the curse. I got mine last year. Don't you remember when I had blood all over the back of my skirt and one of the boys noticed it and teased me? It's okay really, Judy. Really. You're lucky you've got on dark clothing. Here, wad up this toilet paper and stuff it in your knickers. Then go and see Miss Rennie when we get back."

The toilet paper was Jeyes with the harsh consistency of waxed paper, but it was better than having the boys or the masters see me bleeding. It was so awful and I didn't know what it all meant. No one explained this to us, until we got it, that is, and then it was whispered with such an air of shame that somehow it never got passed on to younger girls who didn't have 'it' yet.

When we got back to Silverlands, I went up to see Miss Rennie.

"Well, lassie, you're growing up." She said, "You'll be getting this once a month now. Remember today's date because in four weeks or so, you'll be bleeding again. All we women get this. Some people call it the curse, some say getting your period. The medical name is *menses,* which is Latin for month. You may have some cramping, maybe not. If you have cramps, let me know and I'll let you either have an aspirin or a hot water bottle. Now, here is a box of sanitary napkins and a belt."

She handed me a blue box with twelve long white pads in it. Taking out one pad, she showed me how to secure the long ends of the pad through the belt hooks. She told me how to dispose of the pads when I was done and issued me with some clean navy knickers and shorts, taking my old ones away for the laundry.

That's how they dealt with it! No warning. Wait till you get it and then they'd tell you. And certainly no information about how this monthly bleeding was tied in to our reproductive cycles. It's no wonder that so many of us Silverlands girls either 'had to get married', had abortions, or raised children out of wedlock. How our bodies worked was never explained to us, and we, poor fools, never asked. I'm sure now that if I had asked Kirsten Slater, she would have told me, but I didn't know her very well then.

When the Slaters arrived in April 1955, I was finishing my first year at Perkins and my mother had already gone to Canada. Liz had returned from exile in Chertsey, and not long after the Slaters arrived, Mr. Fraser, having handed over the reins in better order than he found them, left for Scotland and a new job.

More new children arrived during the Slater's first year. The boys were Beverly, Robin and Nick, with Nick's younger brother, Jimmy and another little Nicky going to be fostered by Mrs. Hazell for a year. One nine-year-old girl, Susan, joined us then. She was to stir the hearts, minds and certainly, the prepubescent loins of many of the younger boys for years to come.

> At our three reunions those, now grown, men: the brothers Paul and Nick, Val, Beverly, and Jon, sat around tables with beers in hand and wondered, 'Whatever became of Susan?' Caroline, Liz, Lally and I wondered what it was they had seen in her.

When Kirsten and David Slater arrived, they brought with them the feeling of real family life, with their two little daughters and their deep-seated understanding of children's individual needs. The flat over the garage in the outer courtyard was refurbished for them, to give them time for family life with four year old Becky and two year old Lulu, both of whom looked so like their blonde Danish mother. David, who had met Kirsten at college in Denmark, was tall, dark and bearded. They were a wonderful, warm and friendly couple and, soon after they arrived, they began making positive changes to both our physical and emotional lives.

Before the Slaters, we slept in dormitories – four, five or six to a room, depending on the room's size – our iron bedsteads lined up along the walls. What few clothes we had were kept in baskets on the shelves in the linen closet/sewing room and distributed once a week. Our school uniforms were hung in large wardrobes, one in each room, and the minute we got home from school, we had to change into play clothes. There was just one chest of drawers in every dormitory, in which each of us had a drawer for our few personal things. The girls still slept in the main bedrooms on the first floor front, in those rooms papered with the big rose-patterned wallpaper that we all remember so vividly. Matron's room was at the end of the corridor. The boys slept in the old bachelors' wing, behind the front hall, under the eye of the resident housemaster. Most of the under-staff members slept on the top floor under the roof.

With the Slaters came an unheard of concept – privacy. Cubicles were constructed in each bedroom: simple partitions, about six feet high and painted white, separated each bed and formed a small enclosure. We each had a thin, colorful curtain we could pull across the entrance for even greater privacy. Liz, Caroline, Janet and I were in the big bedroom on the right, after you turned left from the back stairs. *During my research, I learned that Wickens of Chertsey constructed all the cubicles for the dormitories for the grand sum of £388.10s, and the curtains for the cubicles cost £94.1s.8d. 1956 prices!*

Next, our old iron bedsteads and horsehair mattresses were exchanged for brand new beds with wooden headboards and inner spring mattresses. We were each issued our very own three-drawer dressing table with an attached mirror, where we could now keep our own clothes, – no more linen closet handouts on Saturday evenings, we were all issued with changes of underwear and two or three sets of play clothes, still second hand, but made more personal this way. I had a small desk, so that I could study and do the hours of homework I brought home from Perkins. My cubicle had a window overlooking the rhododendron bushes. Liz was in the cubicle behind the door. She doesn't remember ever having any homework or a desk, but she does remember being mad because Janet and I got the windows.

Mavis, the oldest now Ann had left, was the titular head girl and had the little room where once, years before, my sister and her room-mates had taken turns looking through the key hole at a previous head girl dallying with a former assistant housemaster. Mavis, who always seemed so grown-up, never did anything nearly so naughty. I don't remember when she came or left, or even where she went to school. I do know that when she left, she changed both her names and wanted nothing more to do with any of us, afterwards.

Helen Dixon arrived from New Zealand, joined Miss Rennie as her assistant and stayed on as Matron, for a while, after Miss Rennie left in 1956. Miss Rennie had been with us for more than four years, longer than any other Matron, even 'Matey' Irvine. With her Scots accent and her no-nonsense manner, she was a force to be reckoned with, but I believe she was liked by all of us. Helen Dixon was a blond young nurse who was comfortable to be around and easy to talk to, very different from Miss Rennie. She didn't really seem like any matron I had ever known.

Shortly after the Slaters arrived, a new housemaster, an attractive Welshman, David – called Dai – Roberts came. He and David Slater started a pre-school for the littlest ones at Silverlands until eventually all the children went out to school; the very youngest going to Lyne Primary as I had done, so many years before. They had a new younger teacher there now and modern w.c.s had been installed inside the school building.

Around this time, my aunt Audrey gave me a Brownie box camera for my birthday and I began to take photographs, recording memories of my last years at Silverlands and our holidays at the seaside.

As we always had, we continued to go for a holiday to the seaside for two weeks every summer. The year he and Kirsten arrived, David Slater came with us to Margate. He remembers going into the bathroom to take a bath at our lodgings and, upon seeing the tub full of water, thought, "How nice, someone has drawn a bath for me." He leapt in, only to discover that the bathtub had been filled with bleach to remove stains. He got out again, very fast. The following two summers, he accompanied us to Broadstairs and Skegness and was extra careful when taking a bath.

Late in 1956, Noël Coward had left England for Jamaica, Laurence Olivier took over as President of the Fund and Richard Attenborough became Chairman. In the mid-nineteen fifties the number of children in the care of the Orphanage had dwindled from more than fifty to around thirty. The Committee, at David Slater's suggestion and with Attenborough's encouragement, approved a new policy for the way Silverlands was to be run. New staff members would be hired to head up new, smaller 'family' groups within the house.

Meanwhile, for those children whose parents had always wanted to keep them but couldn't afford it, subsidies were provided and they went home. The brothers, Paul and Nick, left when their mother married again and their new stepfather adopted them; Margaret's littlest brother, Graham, went home, too. Christopher, at eighteen, had finished his education at Woking Grammar and went out into the wide world.

Under this new arrangement, the Slater family moved into the main house, to the flat which had served as Miss Rennie's old infirmary and sick room at the top of the front hall stairs, and where, years before, Mrs.

Aggitter had whacked our little bottoms with bamboo canes. Those days were long gone, thank goodness.

We children were divided into three family groups of mixed ages, with boys and girls together, each group with a house parent. This was intended to resemble 'normal' family life for us. Betty Parker, who had been a substitute matron, arrived to head her family group in the former boys' wing. Several of the girls; the new arrivals Susan and Sarah, moved there; and some of the boys, including Raymond (known as Beefy), Terry, Robin, Jonny and his brother Dave, plus a few whose names I don't remember, stayed put. With the newly acquired furnishings, Mrs. Parker and her sons, Colin and Nigel, and later a young au pair named Juta, lived with about ten "orphans" in that wing, along with Mrs. Parker's two Pekinese dogs, Wan Su and Precious Amber.

On the top floor, where the under-staff members used to sleep, Mr. and Mrs. Pilling came to live with us. They were an older couple with no children of their own; she had worked as a cleaner and he as an odd job man. About eight boys and girls lived with them: Gay, her brother Bill, Margaret and Ronnie and Liz until she left. Janet and I stayed where we had always been, joined by Lally and Gaynor.

Caroline was not assigned to any family group. My close companions and life-long friends were to leave that year. Caroline left, a few months before Liz, just after she turned fourteen that March. Early one morning, she was woken up and told by Mr. Slater,

"Get up and get dressed, Caroline. You are going to live with your mother."

This was the first time she knew of it. She packed a small suitcase, was taken to Chertsey and put on the train for Waterloo. There, as she had been instructed, she stood under the clock and waited for her mother. *Years ago, you could do stuff like that!* Caroline waited and waited and waited, but no one came. Apparently, there is more than one clock in Waterloo Station and Caroline was waiting under the wrong one. But eventually, her mother contacted the police and they found each other. Caroline went north to Lancashire to live with her mother and stepfather.

For the next nine years, until she married her longtime boy friend, Caroline stayed with her mother and stepfather, as they went from job to job, and slept

in many different and strange places. I didn't see her again until twenty years later, when she came to America to visit Liz and the three of us got together at my house, drank copious cups of tea, moved on to wine, and talked for hours.

Why they never told any of us where Caroline had gone remains a mystery to me. After all, by this time the staff talked about lots of things, especially to the older kids. But Caroline was gone. Just like that. It left a big hole in my world and an air of uncertainty.

Liz, now sixteen, lived on the top floor with the Pillings group until she finished school that summer and went up to London. Rutland Gate wasn't an option for her, it had closed in 1954 and, her father and step-mother told her she couldn't live with them, so Liz got a job as a secretary (she'd learned to type at school), found a tiny flat in Streatham and, as she says, *"I muddled along until I got the hang of the outside world."* She sometimes came to Silverlands on weekends and slept wherever there was an empty bed. *Liz came to New York City as an au pair in 1964 and found me. We've been there for each other ever since.*

Kath Dutton, who had been one of our cooks for a short time, returned to be my housemother. Kath was an attractive, vivacious divorcee with two little girls, Jackie and Janice, the same ages as Becky and Lulu Slater. 'Mummy' Kath, as she came to be called, moved into the former matron's room at the other end of the first floor from my room. Jackie and Janice had the small dressing room next to her. In the big corner bedroom, now partitioned with cubicles, were two new little sisters, Sally and Fran, Norma and Lally. The two small boys little Nicky and Jimmy shared a room. My roommates were Janet and Gaynor. Older boys Carl, Nick and Bernard moved up to our floor, joined by Mike (a later arrival) and shared a cubicled room, the same size as ours but further down the hall. Every effort was made to keep siblings together. *My memory is muddy as to exactly who was in what group, especially since we still got together at meals and were always in and out of each other's group sitting rooms.*

Later on another au pair girl, sweet Danish Birgitte, came to help Kath and also work in the kitchen. Birgitte said to me at our first reunion, "I was only at Silverlands for nine months compared to your thirteen years, Judy, and yet it was a very important part of my life, so I can imagine how much it meant to you." I told Birgitte that she had been there during the good times: making life-long friends with co-workers and going on dates with the old boys, who still came down on weekends.

Birgitte died of cancer at home in Denmark, not long after that first reunion.

In each family group, we had our own sitting rooms but we still played games and had joint activities in the common rooms downstairs. We ate together as a family group in the dining room and if we had any problems we went to our house parent. David Slater was the court of last resort.

It was a fairly successful attempt to normalize our lives, although we were still at times a rowdy and undisciplined bunch of kids. For the first time in my life, we older girls went to Marks and Spencer's department store in Staines with Kath Dutton and Betty Parker and they let us choose our very own pretty underwear *and* a new jersey each. We now went shopping and on other outings in the newly acquired minibus, usually driven by David Slater, who confessed to me that the staff used the travel time to listen to our chatter and find out what was bothering us – or what villainy we were plotting1

Suddenly, we were being treated as individuals with likes and dislikes, differing problems and specific tastes.

We still had to do chores on Saturday morning. The big boys still shoveled coal and coke for the furnace and worked outside, while the older girls sorted laundry, helped in the kitchen and dusted the main common rooms. Mrs. Minns came in to do the heavier cleaning. Within each family group we pitched in to make our own living quarters homier. We learned to sew a little and to cook appetizing food. We played all kinds of board games and were encouraged to listen to the latest pop tunes on a new electric Victrola: Paul Anka singing *Diana*, Pat Boone's *April Love* and The Kingston Trio's *Hang Down Your Head Tom Dooley* and we all went mad for hula hoops, just as if we were ordinary kids. A memory of those two little boys, Nicky and Jimmy singing *"Don't know what they're doing but they laugh a lot behind the green door'* loudly and off-key, still makes me smile.

Kirsten and David Slater were in charge of the day-to-day running of the house, and they oversaw the staff members who Patrick Waddington had hired.

Kirsten said, "Patrick Waddington was always very keen on engaging new staff members, but if they turned out not to be suitable, then it fell to us to fire them."

She added, "We did not like that part at all!"

She remembered Mrs. Isaacs and her small child, who lasted only ten weeks, and Mrs. Webb, who Mr. Waddington had hired to be head of one family group, and who turned out to be quite deaf. The young European au pair girls came and went.

Sometimes, Mr. Waddington found a real gem. After Miss Rennie left, and Helen Dixon was promoted to Matron, Nurse Inge arrived to assist her and to help in the kitchen. Tall and angular with a rather horsey face, big teeth and untidy, short dark hair, she wore her white nurse's uniform and starched cap most of the time. With her came her small daughter, Cordula. Cordy was four years old when they arrived and she quickly became one of the growing number of little girls and Inge herself became a much-loved member of the household. She was Jewish, although that meant nothing to us, and had been widowed not long before she arrived. I learned many years later that she and her husband, after being liberated from the concentration camps in Germany, had met and married in a Displaced Persons' camp. Her husband had died of war-related injuries leaving Inge with little Cordy. I can still see Inge's lovely, homely face as she stooped to talk earnestly to me, with her pronounced German accent, about some pain I was having. Nurse Inge helped me through some dark times when I had no idea what truly dark times were and she so obviously did.

Inge died of cancer not long after Silverlands closed and Betty Parker's son Nigel adopted Cordy, who is now married and lives in Australia.

My sister had, by this time, left to join our mother in Canada. After Rutland Gate had closed, Sue had stayed with Mother for a short time, sleeping on the couch in the sitting room, until Mother sold the house and left for Toronto. Sue was then boarded with some friends of Mother's in London to finish her training at the Arts Educational School. Mother had also appointed her cousin, John Coast, to be Sue's guardian in England but, after a year of worrying about Sue, who was man-crazy and running wild, he cabled Mother and said he was putting Sue on a plane for Toronto, he could do no more.

Sue lived with Mother in Toronto for a little while. In 1957, Mother was producing a summer season at the Grand Theatre in London, Ontario. Sue joined the company to appear in several plays. It was while they were playing mother and daughter in *The Reluctant Debutante* that Father, in Canada on business and seeing an announcement in the newspaper, went to see a performance. Sue had no idea he was in the audience. He told her, some years later, that he was adhering to the strict restraining order, still in effect at that time, and did not dare make himself known to her. Father had kept track of Sue through Arthur and Monica and, hearing she was in Canada, sought her out. She wept when he told her that he had seen her in *The Reluctant Debutante*.

After that season at The Grand Theatre, Sue joined the Canadian Players and went on tour with them. Returning to Toronto, she met her first husband Jim, left the company and gave up acting to marry him and soon became a mother. Father sent her a telegram from England on her twenty-first birthday. It said 'I am allowed to see you now.' She and her Scottish husband returned to England. Naturally, she wanted to spend as much time as she could with her newly found father. Jim, being rather homophobic and constantly left to mind the baby, left her and took their baby son to Scotland to live with his parents.

Her marriage over, she tried to get her life back together in London, only to have Father die a short year later from a beating by his much younger, and rather unsavory, lover. Sue was devastated by Father's sudden death. I, working in New York and only eighteen, was never to meet him, and treasure the only letter he wrote to me.

With my sister, gone to Canada, I was feeling abandoned yet again. I was now a teenager and inwardly rebelling. I went through mood swings and periods of dark depression, convinced that my mother simply didn't want me and never had. Instead of ignoring me, or telling me to "buck up," the Slaters and Kath Dutton were at once sympathetic and practical. They put me in charge of the four little girls and two littlest boys in my family group. Every morning, I was to help them get dressed and ready for breakfast. When I got home from school, I had to keep an eye on them, sit amongst them at high tea, see to their baths, read them bedtime stories and tuck them in, before I could tackle my homework. I was so busy with Jackie, Janice, Sally, Fran, Jimmy and Nicky I didn't have time to feel sorry for myself.

Often my six charges became nine on weekends when Becky, Lulu and Cordy joined the group down by the swings and in the sandpit, which had, happily, replaced Mr. Fraser's chicken runs. David Slater dug the holes for the swings and excavated a play area in the hillside, which was filled with clean sand (soon to get dirty). Any real toys were soon supplemented with bits of junk that the little kids scavenged. Tin cans, old buckets, rusty cooking pots and even an old iron bedstead, all found their way to the sand pit. Young Nicky remembers being very upset when he arrived and learned he had to share his toys with everyone. The swings were a great hit with us all, big and little, and there were death-defying feats as the daredevils made the swings to go so high and flip right over the top bar.

Nicky, like many other little boys, had been fostered by Mrs. Hazell until he was five and could come up to the big house. When he moved in, he remembers helping to build a bicycle with one of the older boys. They found an old frame with handlebars and a seat to which they attached couple of wheels – but with no nuts and bolts to hold the wheels on. Nicky sat on the saddle while the older boy pushed him down the back drive. When Nicky said something, the boy said, "I'm not holding you now." That was how Nicky, and probably most of us, learned to ride a bike.

Nicky was, like so many of us, the child of divorced actors visited by his mother or father on alternating Visiting Sundays and crying inconsolably when they left. When Silverlands was slated to close, he went home, happily, to live with his mother.

Sally and Fran, less than a year apart, were on either side of four, the age I had been when I arrived. Their father, a prolific writer of film and television, had parted from their mother when the girls were very small. They were sent to Silverlands. As a tiny girl, Sally suffered from a horrid skin ailment; both water and hot or cold weather caused her skin to crack and bleed, and it was very painful. She had to be bathed each night with oil. My own miseries were forgotten as I swabbed her rough and raw little body with baby oil and cotton wool.

One of the younger boys went missing one Saturday. Not Nicky or Jimmy, as they were with me, but it might have been Gay's brother Bill. The staff and some of the older children searched the house and grounds to no avail. The police were notified. We all searched some more. Then, one of the lost boy's friends had a bright idea and the search party moved to the Big Woods. There he was found, sound asleep with a cherubic smile on his face, his wooden sword at his side, curled up on a pile of leaves, no doubt dreaming of derring-do, in one of our not-so-secret camps.

In early 1957 Patrick Waddington had a rather serious motorcycle accident and, after a stay in the hospital, resigned as General Secretary. Mrs. Hollands replaced him. Dai Roberts also left that year.

With David and Kirsten Slater, Patrick Waddington and Richard Attenborough together effecting changes, life had become something to look forward to. In the summertime, we hosted Open House days, when members of the Committee drove down to Silverlands in their fancy cars – Rolls Royces and Bentleys lined the driveway. They joined in our games, sat and chatted with us and became actively involved in our lives. Our most regular visitors were Richard and Sheila Attenborough, and those three grand Dames of the theatre: Edith Evans, Flora Robson and Sybil Thorndike, along with Jill Esmond and Lorn Loraine, who was still keeping Noël Coward informed. We met lots of other stars of the stage and screen, who came to visit us and see how we lived. Ann Todd came down once with her then husband, film director David Lean. Trevor Howard, Brenda Bruce, Mr. and Mrs. Jack Hawkins and Felix Aylmer all came several times, interested in who we were and how we were doing – some of us were tongue-tied. Douglas Byng drove down in his open sports car and gave us rides up and down the driveway. And I clearly remember all of us playing football with Robert Shaw – the future villain of *From Russia With Love*!

Throughout my childhood, Richard Attenborough, Sheila Sim, and these other famous members of the Committee visited us and became familiar, positive forces in our lives. They continued to arrange for tickets London theatres and cinema. We attended many films that starred

Committee members we had met: *Reach for the Sky* with Kenneth More as Douglas Bader (Kenneth More gave us our confirmation prayer books); *Bridge on the River Kwai* with Jack Hawkins and *Merry Andrew* with Danny Kaye who, while not on the committee, appeared several times in *Night of a Hundred Stars*.

Even more memorable was to actually watch a film being made. In 1958, Attenborough arranged for some of us to watch the filming of *Danger Within* on nearby Chobham Common. He was starring in this film about British soldiers escaping from an Italian prisoner of war camp and invited us to visit the set. We put on our coats and 'wellies' – it was a cold and muddy day – piled into the mini bus and stood near the set watching the action. Some of us were actually standing right behind a door in one scene while the cameras were rolling. Later, a group photo was taken of us with three of the film's stars: Attenborough, Richard Todd and a young Australian matinee idol, Vincent Ball. Kath Dutton, my housemother, and I were very taken with Vincent Ball and thought him quite a dish. Even though we came from the world of actors, we were never blasé.

Sometimes, tickets to the London theatre were arranged for, often on very short notice. The older children and some of the staff would get onto a chartered bus and off we'd go up to London and, arriving at the theatre, troop into the front row seats – seats that the management hadn't been able to sell and needed to fill on opening nights. David Slater and some of us older children went to *Night of 100 Stars – 1957*. Laurence Olivier had hurt his ankle and leaned on a walking stick as he emceed the show. Visiting American film stars Kirk Douglas and Burt Lancaster brought the house down singing *Maybe it's because I'm a Londoner* in rather strange Cockney accents.

We went to the Windsor Horse Shows, to Bertram Mills Circus and every year, as we always had, we went to the Theatre Royal Windsor for the Panto, sitting in the best seats in the stalls, filling three, later only two, rows, where we hissed at the villains and laughed at the Dame. The little kids spent days re-enacting every moment on the small stage in the 'Rec' room.

At Christmastime, everyone now received very nice presents, paid for by the fund so everybody's gift was equal in size, and we were also given the usual postal order from the Committee to put into our Post Office Savings accounts. Those children who went to relatives on Boxing Day, as I did, were given their family presents then. My mother was in America by this time. She was never very good at knowing what we liked and she always sent me something for birthday and Christmas combined. Sue, who was born in July, always got two presents each year. Somehow, it never dawned on Mother that this wasn't very fair, but I honestly think she didn't have a clue about such things.

> *I was newly married in 1964 and spending Christmas with my in-laws. They lived in a lovely house in Hartford, Connecticut where my new father-in-law was a distinguished architect and my mother-in-law, a Mark Twain scholar. On Christmas morning, we all sat around the tree and opened our presents. A small package had arrived from my mother. After a while, with some trepidation, I opened it. Inside, loosely wrapped in used Christmas wrapping paper, were four small books filled with green stamps, the sort you received when you shopped for groceries or filled up your car with gasoline, redeemable at any Green Stamp store in America for a variety of household items. Attached was a note to my husband and I in her familiar hand, "Darlings, you can get yourselves a good bathmat or two with these. Happy Wedding and Happy Christmas" love Joan/Mum and Bob.*
>
> *I thought I would die. I wanted the couch to swallow me up. I'm sure I was red in the face. I stammered to my nice new in-laws that my mother was very busy.... always.*

The best present I ever received from her had been for Christmas 1956. She sent me a bright red, down parka from Canada. It was warm, it had a hood and, best of all it was *brand new*. I was the envy of everyone that winter. Liz offered to give me anything she owned (which wasn't much) to let her wear it for a day. That same Christmas our new President Laurence Olivier came down with Vivienne Leigh and gave us each ten bob. I remember Vivienne Leigh being very pale and delicate looking and speaking to us in a whisper.

The Slaters introduced fancy dress parties for Halloween and other occasions. We all put on make-up and elaborate, borrowed costumes, played Charades and won prizes. Even before the Slaters came, at Halloween we'd always had parties in the Rec room where we bobbed for apples or with hands behind our backs, tried to eat the apples and not the candles, tied together and hanging from a string.

An earlier Halloween, when I was ten or so, I remember us all walking through the woods to Lyne churchyard. There we sat on the tombstones hoping to see ghosts and scare each other. Later, walking back through the woods, I got separated from the rest and was suddenly alone in the dark. I ran, terrified, crashing through the underbrush, towards home. A couple of the boys, those who always teased me, hooted owl noises at me from the bushes as I ran.

Because of my glasses and my small pointy nose, one of those boys had started calling me 'Owly'. He would cup his hands together and blow through them, making a hooting sound whenever I walked by. His constant taunting only compounded my general feeling of insecurity. As a teenager, with my round National Health glasses, straight brown hair and a retainer on my teeth, I wasn't a pretty girl, although I never had pimples – whoever handed out the looks spared me that. The opposite sex always found much fairer game and I didn't have a boyfriend until I went to America.

David Slater encouraged us to take an active role in the local community. At the Lyne Village Fair, we competed in the three-legged, egg-and-spoon and sack races against the village children. We teenagers joined the Youth Club at Lyne Hall, where we had Saturday night dances and we, in turn, hosted dances at Silverlands and invited our local friends. At these dances, I would take off my glasses and sit, ever hopeful, along the wall of the Assembly room, waiting to be asked to dance. If someone did lumber towards me, he might just as well have looked like Quasimodo because I couldn't see more than two feet in front of my face; but if I put my glasses on then the hooting began.

We learned to dance all kinds of dances. We waltzed, foxtrotted and did the Sir Roger de Coverly in preparation for those Saturday night dances, although we usually ended up jitterbugging – Elvis was our new hot idol, although, loyal little Brit that I was, I preferred Cliff Richard. Both David and Kirsten had been folk dancers in Denmark and they taught us Scandinavian dancing. All of us girls *and* boys, dressed in colorful clothes resembling traditional costumes, with much stamping, clapping and twirling, danced at area church fêtes, at Lyne Hall and for our celebrity visitors on Open House days. Folk dancing was enormous fun and even two left-footed Judy mastered the steps.

At Lyne Hall, we Silverlanders showed off our theatrical heritage by putting on a rather good production of *The Glass Menagerie*. Gerry, by this time a visiting old boy, played Tom, Mavis was a surprisingly moving Amanda and Mike, the new boy, played the Gentleman Caller. Sarah played Laura and because she was madly in love with Mike at the time, it worked quite well for the play. I helped out backstage.

We were also encouraged to mix with local children and invite them to stay at Silverlands on a weekend. Some even went with us to the seaside in the summer holidays. Suzella and her sister Linda came with us to Skegness and Lillian went to Broadstairs. Suzella had become my friend through the Youth Club; she lived quite near Silverlands, on the Longcross road, and her parents were always very welcoming when I went to visit.

At Lyne church, Vicar Hodge, so despised by Mr. Waddington, had moved on to aggravate another congregation and the new vicar was an easy-going man, the Reverend R.B.T. Gardener. We all returned to Lyne for Sunday services. No more embarrassment for the publican of The Otter. No more six-mile walks to and from Ottershaw. We were back at Lyne, swelling the congregation and making a loud and joyful noise to the Lord every Sunday morning. Some of us joined the choir, had choir practice once a week, and sang at Morning Prayer and Evensong. Our choir mistress was a good musician and fairly innovative for that time, – I remember singing Calypso carols one year, – but she had a two-foot-long finger with which she would jab us between the shoulder blades if we whispered or were giggling at the men from Botleys, especially the one with the naked lady necktie.

We took part in the Christmas and Easter pageants and, at the annual Church Fête, we helped out at the White Elephant table, at the Tombola, at the guessing games ('How many marbles in this jar? Win ten bob!') and at that most popular attraction, the China Smashing Booth. Actually, it wasn't called the China Smashing Booth, I've forgotten what it was really called, but that is what it was. People donated their old china, chipped dinnerware, busted flowerpots, chamber pots, and etcetera. We set it up on stands and for threepence, you got three chances to throw wooden balls and see how much china you could smash. There were no prizes, just the satisfaction of smashing china to smithereens.

There was also, every year, a fancy dress competition with the winner getting a cash prize. Young Nicky remembered this one:

> Learning of the fancy dress competition when we arrived, we were fired with enthusiasm and a couple of us scoured the fete for things we could dress up in. It was not a success. By the time of the judging, all we had managed to find were some feathers which we wore Red Indian fashion in our hair, and our shirts and shorts. We added a little war dance, whooping and singing and stamping. What the good people of Lyne thought of this I dread to think, however the competition was won by a girl who was entered as 'An English Country Garden.' She wore a shiny, ground length dress flared at the bottom and painted in greens and browns (I suppose to look like a tree) with a similar hood. It was so tight around her knees that she couldn't walk and had to be carried into position by her father. Hanging from her neck, like an usherette's ice cream tray, was a beautifully constructed model garden. She could not possibly have dressed herself or created that garden! As soon as she appeared, there was no doubt in my mind that she would win and the prize that we had hoped for slipped from our over-confidant grasp. The judges awarded us some sweets for our efforts and we were pleased with that. But I learned at the age of five or six that there are always people who are better placed in life and have the background, support, confidence and means to achieve whatever they set out to do, with or without the talent to do it.

On Rogation Sundays, we traipsed through mud and puddles, wearing our 'wellies' and 'macs', following Vicar Gardener around a neighboring farm while he blessed every field and each cow and chicken. The whole congregation straggled along behind him singing *We plow the fields and scatter*. At Harvest Festival, we brought vegetables from the Silverlands gardens to pile in front of the altar, to be distributed to needy families. Not for us any more!

One year, our little Lyne choir was chosen to sing in the Diocesan Festival at the new Guildford Cathedral. We were among twenty choirs participating. We arrived in chartered buses to the big yellow imposing, but rather ugly, cathedral on top of Stag Hill. There, all twenty choirs sang Brahms' *Requiem* and watched the Bishop of Guildford celebrate Holy Communion.

In May of 1958, the Bishop, himself, came to Lyne and confirmed Terry, Mike, Bernard, Kenny, Sarah, Margaret, Gay, Gaynor and me, along with several of the Lyne children. When it was my turn to go up to the altar, I walked slowly, dressed all in white with my head covered in a long white piece of cloth. As I reached the hassock, placed in front of the Bishop, I knelt down carefully but I was just a little too far forward and pitched straight into his lap. He confirmed me anyway. At least, he signed the paper saying he had. I don't really remember what happened or how I got out of his lap. I was too embarrassed.

By now, Mr. Slater had become very involved in church activities. As a lay reader, he was occasionally called upon by Reverend Gardner to preach a sermon. During one of his sermons, Janet leaned over and whispered something in Sarah's ear. Complete pandemonium followed, as Sarah, in his words, 'went half-potty.' Mr. Slater later learned that Janet had whispered the provocative words, "I'm pregnant," which of course she wasn't.

Sarah had arrived at Silverlands late in 1956. She was taller than Margaret, Gay and I, even though she was the same age, and she positively towered over Liz. She was also very well developed and she wore a bra long before any of us did; much to our envy and the boys' lustful delight. She had slightly protruding front teeth and mane of heavy, straight brown hair that she would spend hours brushing. With quite a flare for the dramatic, Sarah could be relied upon to spread any rumor. She claimed to be a direct descendant of Charles Dickens and I heard that she went into the theatre for a while after she left, but we have lost touch with her.

Some of the latest arrivals were very young like Sally, Fran and Nicky, a few like Sarah, Chris and Mike were older. With the days at Silverlands drawing to a close, none of these newcomers would be living with us for long.

FIFTEEN

Silverlands for Sale

The news appeared in *The Stage* on 15 May 1958

ACTORS' ORPHANAGE MAY LEAVE SILVERLANDS.
The Actors' Orphanage may be moving from Silverlands, said
the vice-President, Richard Attenborough, at the annual general
meeting of the Fund at the Saville on May 6, when he read the
chairman's report at the request of the chairman, Nicholas Hannen.

Mr. Attenborough explained that many difficulties had
presented themselves at Silverlands. The financial ones included
the necessity for renewing and enlarging the oil-heating plant and
urgent repairs to the roof, which would total something in the
region of £15,000. In addition to this, and no less important, were
staffing difficulties caused by the isolated position of the house.

The family group system, introduced a year ago, had proved
beneficial to the children, but its success was threatened by
the difficulty of engaging and retaining the services of suitable
house mothers in a region so far from the amenities of a town.
It was essential to the welfare of the children that there was a
feeling of permanence about the family group system, and as
things were, this might be in danger of collapsing. The decision
to move away from the countryside amenities of Silverlands had
not been taken lightly.

"But cutting down on our running costs, which is the expected
result of this move, and by keeping up our efforts to raise money,"
said Mr. Attenborough, "it is hoped that we may in the future
be able to subsidize some needy children in their own homes and
so save families from being split up. This is surely a better way of

spending money than upon roof repairs!"

Mrs. Hollands (General Secretary replacing Mr. Waddington) reported that the children liked the family group system and that it has been found this makes it easier to maintain discipline and to give individual attention to the problem children who are emotionally disturbed by the break-up of their homes. Most of the children in the Fund's care were not orphans. No new children had been admitted in the past year, added Mrs. Hollands, and thirteen boys and girls had left, leaving 29 now in the care of the orphanage. There had been a steady drop in numbers over the past six years, due either to the benefits of the Welfare State or to fuller employment in the theatrical profession.

Parents and guardians had been notified as to whether they would like their children come and live with them and, if they would, they would be eligible for a monthly assistance cheque. (The Actors' Charitable Trust still supports these needy families). Those parents who could not, *or would not*, take their children were assured that, when Silverlands closed, the children would be re-settled in two small family groups under the continuing care of Mr. and Mrs. Pilling and Mrs. Parker in two small houses in Watford.

Immediately after this announcement, there was a great deal of coming and going. Some of the children left almost immediately, as soon as school was over, now that there were subsidies available. James left to live with his parents and sister, his younger brother Andrew following soon after. The older Nick and his brother Paul had left already: Paul went on to work behind the scenes in film and television and Nick moved to New Zealand where he became a wing commander in the New Zealand Air Force. Derek, who had been sent to a sanitarium in Switzerland as a cure for his asthma and suspected tuberculosis, returned to Silverlands for the final year before moving on.

Some, who had come within the last four years after Gordon, would complain as adults, as Gay had, how the harshness of life at Silverlands had affected them. *They didn't know what harshness was!* Some children, who had arrived just before Attenborough's announcement, were gone again before we got to know them, to rejoin their parents now that financial help was available.

Easily the strangest arrival and departure was that of little Kevin. One day in the autumn of 1955, a couple of years before either Liz or Caroline had left, Mr. Waddington took them for a drive. In the car, he told them they were going to fetch their little brother, Kevin, and bring him back to live with them. They were stunned, until that moment, they had no idea that they had a brother! Mr. Waddington explained carefully that Kevin was their mother's son, but not by their father or stepfather. He had been placed by their mother in another charity home in Sussex since infancy, and was now old enough to come to Silverlands. Kevin, a small blond boy, lived at Silverlands for a few years, until a Welsh couple saw him on Adoption Parade and gave him a new home. Caroline and Liz left shortly before Kevin, never knowing what had become of this little brother they never really got to know.

The Slaters, too, would be moving on once everyone was resettled. David's growing interest in serving the Church had led to his decision to attend King's College to study theology. Eventually, he was ordained a priest and, after serving in several parishes, he became a Canon of the Church of England and was appointed Vicar to the Close of Salisbury Cathedral – the very same Cathedral where my great grandfather had sung in the choir.

On 14 June 1958, the summer before the Slaters and almost everyone left, Kirsten, who we had all watched become bigger and bigger in her pregnancy, gave birth to Simon in their flat at Silverlands. When Simon was only a few hours old, we were invited up to their little flat to visit Kirsten with the tiny baby in her arms. The Slaters made us feel a part of this, letting us all share in their family event, and Kirsten's look of happiness that day stays with me still.

During the summer many children left for home: Margaret and Ronnie left. Gay and Bill went to live with their mother in London and finished their education there. Carl, who had arrived just a year after I did, went north to Glasgow, where his family came from. Little Nicky, one of my small charges, went home and so did Robin, David, Mavis and my old friends, the twins Janet and Bernard.

Terry – not Terry Mac, he'd long since left – left to live with his mother and sister. He had applied for a job at a London bank. He wasn't quite sure what a job interview was all about, but he got the job anyway. He used to come down for weekends, until everyone moved on. He was a nice lad Terry, always had something good to say about everyone. Eventually he moved to Canada, roomed with Ed for a while, married Lynne and adopted two Korean orphans. He worked his way up the banking ladder in Canada, before retiring. Many of the boys, in their reminiscences, remember Terry warmly. Ray wrote to me,

> Terry taught us how to spin a tennis ball on your finger,
> helped us with our homework and, it was he who always
> organized everyone's football uniforms, making sure
> they were clean and ready for the next game.'

Terry used to spend endless hours on the platform at Chertsey station collecting train numbers or standing along the roadside with his little notebook writing down car and bus license plates. Numbers were always Terry's passion and so, perhaps logically; banking and numbers became his life.

Those two blond brothers of different fathers, Jonny, whose photo had been taken all those years ago with Marlene Dietrich, and Dave, who was so harshly mistreated by Gordon, went home to their mother. She had married a good and kind man who adopted both boys and gave them love and guidance. Dave died far too young.

After our first reunion in Chertsey in 2000, I had returned to America and received an e-mail from the Noël Coward Society asking me if I had grown up with a boy named Jonny (no surnames here) . I replied, yes I had and I would love to hear from him. They gave him my address and phone number. He called and we learned, to our amazement, that he had been living just fifteen miles from me for the past seven years. I called Liz, who was living an hour further south in the Hudson River Valley. The three of us got together. Jon had three fine sons and been divorced once, like so many of us. Jon and Liz were married in 2009 and at their Mississippi wedding at the home of Liz's son, I told the

invited guests the story of how we three first met. Jon and Liz are living
together again, after fifty years, but in a much smaller house in America.

The move to Watford had been planned for early January, 1959. Norma,
Lally, Gaynor, Sarah, Fran and little Sally were the girls; Beverly, Chris,
Mike, Nick and his brother Jimmy were the only boys to go. Ray did go to
Watford for a bit but, being a bright lad, was sent to Lindisfarne boarding
school in Wales for four years to finish his education (paid by the Fund).

Ray had been a tough little boy when he arrived in 1951 at five. He
earned the nickname 'Beefy', although he wasn't at all really, he was resilient. He soldiered on through Berry, Gordon, Fraser and the Slaters,
always meeting everything and everyone head-on.

After Lindisfarne, Ray went to art school in London and then
immigrated to Australia 'on a Pommy's pound.' In Sidney he met and fell
in love with Anne from Tasmania. They married and live in Tasmania,
still. Ray, after drawing geographical surveys, is now happily retired,
gardening and devoted to his family. He turned up again, like so
many of us wandering orphans, because he, too, had contacted the Noël
Coward Society when he reached middle age and started wondering
what had become of everyone. They gave him my address.

Why it was Mr. and Mrs. Pilling, and not Kath Dutton, who were put
in charge of one of the Watford houses, I do not know. When Juta, one
of the au pairs, told me that Mr. Pilling had made unwelcome advances
to her and she had had to fight him off – then surely he was not a suitable house parent, especially for young girls. Gay and Margaret had both
been in the Pillings family group, up on the top floor. That last spring,
both girls had asked Mr. Slater could they please move out of the Pilling's
group and into the now empty room over the courtyard archway, under
the bell tower. Gay, being my best friend and schoolmate at the time, had
asked if I could sleep up there with them. Permission was granted, but
we still had to join our family groups for meals. By this time, I was in the
Lower Fifth form and my homework load had increased. O levels were
looming but Birgitte had arrived and relieved me of my responsibility to
all the little ones.

For those final three months in the tower room, both Gay and Margaret seemed upset about something and kept saying how Mr. Pilling was creepy; but they wouldn't say more than that. After they left Silverlands, both of them went through difficult times emotionally. I am sure that they, neither of whom had lived through the trauma of Gordon or the early post-war years, had nevertheless had another kind of traumatic experience. Both Gay's mother and Margaret's parents wanted to have their children come home and not go to Watford, and so home they both went at the end of that last summer. While I did stay in touch with Gay for many years, I lost touch with Margaret.

So there it was. By the end of that summer, many of the children had returned home and just a dozen or so remained. They were to move in January to newly purchased houses, Rookwood and Nascott Wood, in Watford. Everyone but me!

What was to happen to me?

That winter term, I was in the upper fifth form at Perkins and about to take those O-levels – important for those intending to apply for university. My only known parent, my mother, was three thousand miles and almost five years away.

My father, although possibly still alive, was an absence rather than a presence – mind you, he was a strong absence. Some Silverlands children had fathers who were often out of work or parents who were divorced, but at least they knew their fathers. Other kids had well-known actor-fathers who simply didn't acknowledge them, often because they had been born of illicit relationships. My father was neither an illicit relationship nor an out of work actor; he was a goner – not dead, just gone. Gone before I was old enough to even realize or appreciate what a father might be. Just gone.

My mother wrote that she had recently married again, this time to an American set designer eighteen years her junior. He was teaching at Rollins College in Florida and she was touring America as Mrs. Higgins in the National Company of *My Fair Lady*.

It was decided that I should stay on at Perkins and finish out the school year. Then I would move to Watford the following year, when I would be in the Sixth Form, take my A levels and train to be a nurse, when I was 18. A nurse is what they said I had thought I would like to be, when asked by some ladies of the Committee on one of their visits. Actually, I don't think I ever knew what I wanted to be, but once you told them what you thought you might like to be when you grew up – because you had to come up with something, – there was no changing your mind. That was it! We were definitely career-tracked. Some boys to the army or air force; Ed to the Merchant Navy; Terry was good at arithmetic and so to banking he must go. We girls were to either become secretaries, nannies, nurses or teachers. All of us, boys and girls, were strongly discouraged from working in The Theatre.

A suitable family was sought, one willing to put me up, and put up with me, until the school year was over. Barbara Millman had worked in the theatre as a property mistress in her younger days, she knew Mother and Audrey slightly and she offered to have me board with her family in nearby Staines, in return for remuneration, of course. And so, from January until July of 1959, for those final months of my formal education, I was uprooted from the only home I ever knew and went to live, like a fish out of water, in an ordinary one-family, semi-detached row house in Staines.

Staines was a most fitting name for the dreary town it was in the fifties. It was about five miles and three railway stations north of Chertsey. After living in a 27-room Georgian mansion for most of my life, this depressingly ordinary row house, on an insignificant street, was quite a let down. Mr. and Mrs. Millman were nice enough people and she especially tried very hard to make me feel at home. She had decorated a tiny room under the roof with pink wallpaper covered with little sprigs of flowers. The bed was soft and comfortable with a pink and white chenille counterpane and *two* pillows. I had a desk, a small cupboard for my clothes, a bedside lamp and a small white radio of my very own. But I was feeling much too displaced to really appreciate any of it. I had lived most of my life in a dormitory with a large wardrobe in which there were a couple of pegs to hang my few clothes on, and I had slept, until relatively recently, on a thin horse-hair mattress under scratchy sheets and one very thin blanket. I was unused to comfort and solitude.

Mr. Millman was an invalid with emphysema and a bad heart. He had once been a car salesman and now spent his days in an armchair with a lap robe, listening to the Third Programme on the BBC and whittling shapes from pieces of scrap wood into charming little birds and Noah's Ark animals. Barbara Millman spent her life taking care of his every need and the needs of their spotty son.

This spotty son was not in anyway a replacement for my forty-odd 'brothers and sisters', who were now scattered to the winds: to Watford, to their parents or into the working world. He was overweight, pimply and intellectual. He had big lips and thick glasses and was extremely pompous. With no sense of humour – the word 'fun' was just not in his vocabulary. I doubt if he had ever hung by his knees from trees or let off stink bombs outside a matron's room. All in all, he was altogether the most unappealing specimen of the opposite sex that my eyes had ever seen, and yet Mrs. Millman adored him.

Now, that was a new concept for me, one I didn't know about: a parent adoring a child, especially a child as awful as he seemed to me. But adore him she did. That boy never had to lift a finger. She washed and ironed his clothes, made his bed, turned the radio down while he did his homework and generally treated him as if he were the Prince of Wales. I, on the other hand, helped with the dishes, did my own laundry using Barbara's mangle to wring out my clothes before hanging them on the line, made my own bed and crept about the house in fear that I would disturb the invalid father or the crown prince. My one joy was listening to *The Goon Show* under the bedcovers late at night. Life was miserable in Staines and my marks suffered.

My mother, completely unaware of who I was, received copies of my school reports and decided I needed a tutor. She even offered to pay for one. Both Barbara Millman and Mrs. Hollands felt that I simply needed encouragement. Mrs. Hollands even went so far as to thank my mother for her offer and suggest that if she now had a hundred pounds to spare that she might like to donate it towards my care and feeding. She didn't. (Later, when Mother had returned to live in England, she did make small annual gifts to TACT in memory of my small son.)

Barbara Millman was a good woman and she tried to understand my discomfort. She knew I missed my old life and encouraged me to go "home" to Silverlands for the weekends, while people were still there. I had moved to Staines at the start of the winter term in January 1959. Most of the homeward bound children had left the previous year, and those going on to Watford left when I did. A few old boys and former staff members remained to pack up the house. Every weekend, that I possibly could, I went back to Silverlands and tried hard not to dwell on my disenfranchisement.

That first weekend in April, after everyone had finally moved out, I told Mrs. Millman I was, again, going to Silverlands to say goodbye. Arriving at the main gate I pushed my bike along the path Gay and I had taken so often on our way to school. Dropping my bike and satchel, I climbed up into the beech tree near the Hazells' goat pen. From there I watched as three huge lorries trundled down the driveway loaded with furniture, some of it headed for storage, eventually to go to Denville Hall, my mother's final abode, and some headed for Watford.

When the lorries were gone, I climbed down the tree, picked up my bike and rode down Holloway Hill, along the Guildford Road through Chertsey to the River Thames, where I crossed the old bridge and rode along the towpath to Staines. I told Mrs. Millman I didn't want any supper. She asked if I was ill and I said, no, I was sad. I tried to explain it to her, but she couldn't really understand why it was that I should be sad that the orphanage had closed.

Those last few months at Perkins were a blur. Gay had gone. I went to school by train or bicycle from Staines. I took my O levels and managed to pass only four with any decent marks. The Committee and Mrs. Hollands called me on the carpet and said, "Judy, it just isn't good enough. You will now have to take these exams again next year if you are to get into nursing school and make something of your life."

I didn't care. As far as I was concerned life, as I knew it, was over.

David and Kirsten Slater had sympathized with my doldrums and, to cheer me up, had suggested that I join them in Wales for the summer holidays and help take care of their growing family. Kirsten was pregnant again. The promise of a trip to Wales was like manna from heaven and I wanted so desperately to go. Mrs. Hollands said it was all right with her if it was all right with my other guardian, my aunt Audrey.

Audrey said, "No." She wrote to my mother saying I had an unhealthy crush on Mr. Slater and that it should not be encouraged. Unhealthy crush indeed! Yes, I had a crush on the Slaters – but it was equally divided between the two of them. They were the nearest I had ever had to proper parents. They were leaving my life and had just offered me a sweet holiday. But Audrey was adamant and Mother went along with her and so I didn't go to Wales.

Mother, in an effort to make up for my disappointment, said she would send me a *round-trip ticket* to America for my summer holidays. This way she would see me again and I could meet my new stepfather. In September, I would then return from America and live at Watford until I took and passed more O levels and took the A levels needed for nursing school. I still didn't know if I wanted to be a nurse, but I realized I didn't have much say in the matter.

After school was finally over and goodbyes said, I was taken shopping for some new clothes and a new blue cardboard suitcase. My passport picture was taken and my visa arranged. My flight was to leave late in the evening, so Audrey took me out for a farewell dinner to a fancy Moroccan restaurant in London that she and Michael frequented. There I asked for the *soup du jour*, the restaurant's special delicacy. After tasting it, I asked the waiter, "What are these little round things?" he said, 'Sheep's eyeballs.' I hurried to the ladies room. Even though I had eaten many dodgy meals in my short life, sheep's eyeballs were too much, even for me. Having sicked up my last meal, I was ready to leave England.

SIXTEEN

Coming to America

ON 28 JULY 1959, my aunt Audrey put my suitcase and me on a TWA 707 flight bound for San Francisco, California, where the *My Fair Lady* Company was currently engaged. I had never been near any kind of airplane before and this was a very big one. It would fly over the polar route, refuel in Winnipeg and land in San Francisco eleven hours later. I was perhaps a little nervous about flying, but mostly I was full of a strange kind of anticipation. I didn't know what to expect at the end of the flight. My mother had always caused my emotions to seesaw. I had missed her, but I didn't really know her; I was in awe of her and yet I remembered her too often careless words. Mostly, I thought "This is my big adventure," and I was determined to enjoy it.

Arriving in San Francisco, I presented my passport (the photograph of me in my school uniform made me look as though I had escaped from St. Trinian's) and was welcomed to the United States by a large and friendly customs official, who opened my suitcase, smiled at my old Teddy lying on the top and closed it again, saying,

'You're all set, honey.'

I lugged my suitcase out into the Arrivals area to look for my mother. I hadn't seen her for five years. I had been eleven then. She had been taller than I and, in my memory, she was always very glamourous. All around me were possible mothers. Tall, dyed blond women in cotton frocks and high heels; older ladies in smart suits, coifed grey hair and shiny handbags. I stared at their faces looking for traces of Sue or Audrey or the chic mother I dimly remembered.

Two short ladies in tracksuits and trainers approached and stood looking at me.

"Are you Judy?" one inquired. She was quite three inches shorter than I but looked somewhat like Audrey. "Yes," I said, "Are you my mother?"

I stayed with the *My Fair Lady* Company for six weeks, and I watched that magical musical at every matinee and evening performance. I explored San Francisco and made friends with the Company gypsies (chorus boys and girls). When the Company moved on to Portland, Oregon, Mother said it was time for me to think about returning to England.

Summoning up some backbone I didn't know I had, I said, "I'm not going back, I like it here."

"But what am I going to do with you?" she cried. "I can't keep you with me."

"Don't worry about me," I replied, "I've got my Post Office savings book and I can cash in my return ticket. I'll be alright."

And I was. And I am.

Before the end of Mother's tour with *My Fair Lady*, I stayed with kind friends in New England. Then, when she returned to New York, I slept on a couch in an alcove in my mother and stepfather's apartment on West 49th Street, in Hell's Kitchen, for three months. With the help of new friends, I found a job, a tiny apartment, was fitted for some contact lenses and learned to stand on my own two feet. It was a whole new world and I explored every facet of it.

The following summer, Mother and Bob (stepfather-in-training) were hired to produce a season at The Berkshire Playhouse. I went along, not to stay with them, but to work for them in the box office and I got to play the tiny part of a Scottish schoolgirl in *The Happiest Days of Your Life* with Margaret Hamilton.

The people I met there introduced me to more people. I took singing lessons, got a good job at Equity Library Theatre, was offered a scholarship to study acting with Herbert Berghof in Greenwich Village and, pretty soon, I began to find work in my family's business – The Theatre.

I saw Mother fairly often and even worked with her sometimes, but mostly I made my own way, slowly figuring out how the world worked. Mother and I eventually came to a tacit agreement, she wouldn't have to hear about my childhood and I would stop asking about my father. I looked for love, companionship and comfort elsewhere, sometimes in the wrong places, but often in the right ones.

Susannah back in England by this time, was seeing a lot of our father and working in London – her husband and baby son having gone north to Aberdeen to live with his parents. Sue reminded Father that he had another daughter in America and he wrote me a rather sweet but formal letter, which ended,

> Weather here now is delightful – winter over – spring well advanced – the scents of summer yet to come. I'm always happiest when the sun shines.
>
> I'd like to send you a present for all the birthdays missed. Let me know what you'd like.
>
> Must sign off and remember to post this – so here's to the next time.
>
> Much love. Affectionately, Father.

I wrote back and asked for a long-playing record of the rather off-colour West End review *The Lord Chamberlain Regrets*, which my very gay English costume designer friend, Alan said I simply *must* have. Several weeks later it arrived in the post, along with five-pounds and a very brief note questioning my taste in theatre! That was the last time I heard from him – within months he was dead. I wish now that I had begged or borrowed the money to see him, just once.

After five years in the States working in many different jobs, earning my Actors' Equity card and playing some wonderful character roles, I auditioned for the upcoming Broadway musical *High Spirits*, based upon Noël Coward's *Blithe Spirit*, which would star Beatrice Lillie, Tammy Grimes and Edward Woodward. Noël Coward was directing and they offered me the part of understudy to the maid, Edith. Alas, I was already under contract, as first assistant stage manager and understudy for the roles of Margaret More and the Woman, with the bus and truck tour of *A Man For All Seasons* – my fate was sealed. The management wouldn't let me out of my contract. Terry Fay, the casting director told me,

"Actors are a dime a dozen, but good assistant stage managers who can also understudy character roles are hard to find."

So instead of the chance to work on Broadway, I saw the U.S. of A — thirty-three thousand miles on a bus for six months — and the inside of one hundred and fifteen old vaudeville and movie theatres in small cities and towns all over North America. (We played to eleven people in Casper, Wyoming on the night John F. Kennedy was assassinated.) I fell hard for the actor playing Will Roper, got pregnant, got married (in that order) and when our son Corin was born, I gave up my fledgling acting career to be a full-time mother — I was *never ever* going to put my family before my career. Corin's sister Abby was born a year later.

Corin died in an accident when he was eighteen months old. I fell apart. My mother was also in Manhattan at that time, in rehearsal for John Arden's *Sergeant Musgrave's Dance*. She was, as usual, too busy to give me any comfort, so I turned to my mother-in-law. She and Abby held us together. A year later, we had another little girl, Sherrod. That first marriage, lasting more than eighteen years, gave me two wonderful daughters, a mother in law who showed me what a mother should be, and taught me, now no longer a charity brat, much about life.

Our marriage, which came about because he was 'doing the right thing' by me and I needed love and family, was ultimately not strong enough. After years of fewer and fewer happy times and infidelity on his part, he left me for another woman. Once again, I was standing on my own two feet, but now I had my girls — I had grown up with them during those years. I also had a job and a career in which I felt confident and successful. After the divorce, I supported my family doing public relations and marketing for various arts organizations. Nine years later I married again, this time because I had found someone who was completely right for *me*.

I have survived, thrived and am now living happily ever after because, as Liz always said, "We'll be all right, Judibugs. We can overcome anything. We went to Silverlands."

CODA

THE DAY FOLLOWING our mother's memorial service on Friday, September 10th, 1999, Susannah and I, along with our family friend, Rosemary, went to the Duke of York's Theatre on St. Martin's Lane in the West End. We each carried a small plastic Ziploc bag containing a tablespoon or two of Mother's ashes, which we were going to scatter backstage. (Sue had obtained permission from the Ambassador Theatre Group, the current tenants of the Duke of York's).

At about ten thirty in the morning, we passed through the lobby and entered the darkened theatre. We groped our way down the aisle towards the single work-light standing in the center of the stage – the only illumination. In the gloom, we could just make out, high above the proscenium, the shield on which had once been emblazoned the letters "VM," the initials of Violet Melnotte – *grande dame*, founder and former owner of the Duke of York's. She was part of the reason we were here. Years before, Violet had hired our father, A.P. Moore, to manage her theatre. She had even asked him to marry her, but being fifty years older than he there was an ensuing scandal. Violet, mindful of negative publicity, changed her mind and said she was going to adopt him instead. She died before that could come about. After Violet died, Father met our mother who was appearing in a play at this theatre, now under his sole management. Their wedding reception was held on this very stage. Much sadness had come from their marriage.

It was rumoured among actors that Violet's angry ghost haunted the theatre. Perhaps she had cursed our parents' union from beyond the grave. Our hope was, by scattering Mother's ashes here, they would counteract Violet's malevolent spirit, lift any remaining vestiges of the rumoured curse and, at the same time give Mother a theatre to haunt – if she needed one.

200

Reaching the apron, Sue opened the house door to backstage, and we walked through the wings and onto the set for Conor McPherson's play *The Weir*, an Irish pub.

Rosie took stage right, dribbling ashes around the prompt desk and the Props table. Sue took center stage sprinkling ashes liberally behind the bar. I had stage left. My portion of the gritty ashes fell around the fly ropes and the old sandbagged counterweights. There was the dust of ages back there, the cobwebs seemed to have been woven before the First World War – Mother's ashes were caught in them making a delicate pattern.

We were quickly finished and thanking the stage doorman, the only living soul in the theatre beside ourselves that morning, we exited through the lobby and into the weak sunshine of that September day. Feeling just a little ghoulish, and since it was now past eleven o'clock, we walked up St. Martin's Lane to a nearby pub. Raising her glass of the best Bitter to the dear departed, Sue said she swore she had seen the ghost of Violet out in the orchestra seats while she was ash-scattering.

"Not possible, Sue, " said Rosie, "Violet only shows up at ten o'clock at night to slam doors during performances. I know. I was in a play there a couple of years ago."

We were happy to have left a little bit of Mother at the Duke of York's, where she had been young and carefree, before we were born and Father had left. Her life had changed so dramatically afterwards. She had immersed herself in her career, setting aside her children for other responsibilities. Later, Sue and I would take a small amount of her ashes home with us. My portion is planted in my New York garden under a *Rosa Rugosa*, – a tiny part of her is forever in America where her career flourished for almost thirty years. Sue took her portion to Gibraltar to be scattered over our grandparents' grave, because Mother had grown up in Portugal and Gibraltar before she left for school in England and afterwards sought her fortune as an actress. The rest of her ashes are buried in the corner of our family plot in a country churchyard within sight of Salisbury cathedral where her maternal ancestors had worshipped for centuries. After almost ninety years on this earth, her remains are now laid to rest in the lands where she had lived her long life.

The day before our visit to The Duke of York's, dressed in our best clothes, we held a memorial service for this actress, Joan White, at the Actors' Church in Covent Garden. Sue and Rosie had arranged the event, sent out the notices, ordered the flowers, and invited friends, colleagues and students. Some were invited to remember Mother with short speeches. Richard Syms, an actor *and* a priest, would lead the religious portion of the service. Appropriate music was selected and played. Her family was seated in the front row: two daughters, five of her six grandchildren, and five great grandchildren. I, her American daughter, was to give the Eulogy.

What did I say about a mother who wasn't maternal or motherly, but was a greatly respected actor, director and teacher? About this woman, who could and did set aside her children but who would never have done so to her students or fellow actors? About a woman who had had three husbands, two daughters, eight grandchildren, and seven great-grandchildren all of whom hardly knew her, and yet she had many great and close friends?

No less than eight people stood up and spoke about her and her accomplishments. Former students, musicians and actors, including her former co-star Paul Scofield, all read, sang or praised her life to a packed church. She'd worked with many well-known actors over the years: Robert Donat, Lilli Palmer, Laurence Olivier, and Gladys Cooper, to name just a few. She'd had plays written for her and numbered many playwrights among her closest friends. But it was I who was to write her Eulogy. I, who knew her only as 'Mother,' the only role at which she had not excelled and in which she was least comfortable.

Did I chastise her for her maternal omissions? Did I say that Sue and I had been put aside in order that she might work at her career and eventually be worthy of being eulogized here in the Actors' Church with this gathering of her peers? No, I didn't. My Granny always said, "One must not speak ill of the dead, Ducky." Our mother did what she did because she was a woman of the theatre, and that she did well. For this I am proud of her.

I had decided to speak of her accomplishments as an actress, inserting our entrances into the world as if motherhood was just another role she had signed on to play.

I took my place at the lectern, my prepared notes in front of me, and wearing one of her jaunty little 1940s hats, I looked out at the sea of faces and said:

"It's a full house, Mother," and then I began:

> My mother, Joan White, was cast as Phoebe in the 1936
> film of *As You Like It*, which starred Elisabeth Bergner and
> Laurence Olivier, when she was just 26 years old. George
> Bernard Shaw had spotted her in a performance of *The Black
> Eye*, at The Shaftsbury Theatre and said to Bergner, 'There's
> your Phebe.' As Phebe, she is now immortalized on film:
>
> > Think not I love him though I ask for him
> > 'Tis but a peevish boy, yet he talks well;
> > But what care I for words? Yet words to well,
> > When he that speaks them pleases those that hear.
>
> Good lines for a lady who later became a teacher of speech and
> drama and taught us, her children, the importance of enunciation.
> Shakespeare also wrote 'One man in his time plays many parts.'
> Our mother was a woman of many, many parts. As well as a
> mother, grandmother and great-grandmother, she has been a wife
> – several times – a director, a producer, a teacher to scores, no
> hundreds of students, and an actress in more roles than I can name.
>
> For the first fifteen years of her long career she played
> teenagers: *Little Ladyship* (while pregnant with my sister);
> *Susannah and the Elders* (from which my sister got her
> name); *House Master* with her classic line 'Do you mean
> funny peculiar or funny ha-ha?' and as thirteen year-old
> Judy Graves in *Junior Miss* when, at thirty-four, she had
> just given birth to a ten pound eight ounce baby – me!'

And on I went, covering her long career in the theatre, telling little anecdotes, never mentioning us, her children again, and ending with this:

> One of her last performances was for the BBC television
> production of *The Singing Detective* as old Mrs. Adams.
> Fortunately this, too, is preserved on film so now future
> generations will be able to see her enormous range as an actress
> – from Phebe to Mrs. Adams some sixty years later.
> My godfather, Sir Tyrone Guthrie, who was her friend
> and mentor, gave Mother her start both in England with the
> Cambridge Festival Theatre Company in 1930 and in Canada
> in 1954. He also gave our indefatigable mother her motto
> 'Rise Above It' and so she did, whenever life got her down.
> She certainly has now, she's up there somewhere not waiting
> in the wings but waiting for her wings. Cheerio, Mum.

After several more speeches, poems and songs, the congregation exited the church with great amusement to the strains of Noël Coward's *Don't Put your Daughter on the Stage, Mrs. Worthington*. We then regrouped around the corner at Mother's club, The Green Room, for warm whiskey, cheap wine and hors d'oevres, which are now called 'Starters' only these were 'Afters.'

Through writing this memoir, I have come to terms with the feelings I had for my late mother and, tangentially, for my sister. To an outsider it might seem as though I, as the daughter left behind at the Actors' Orphanage, was the one hard done by. But in truth, if things had been different, I might well have had the topsy-turvy life my sister has had. She spent her early adult years looking hard and long for love, as many of us did, and in so doing entered into too many marriages to men who were not what she needed. Later in her life, she reconciled with her children and became happier and more settled.

Our mother was a fine actor and director and, I am told by her many students, she was a caring and conscientious teacher. As a fellow theatre professional I admired her, but I cannot honestly say I loved her. Perhaps, she simply lacked the maternal gene – if there is such a thing.

I have learned that you make your family where you find it and I wanted this book to try to convey something of what that means. Kirsten and David Slater, who came to Silverlands *in loco parentis* for my last five years, have remained so ever since. Many former Silverlands children I still think of as my brothers and sisters. Most have done well in their lives: marrying, raising families and pursuing careers. Some died far too young. Inevitably, there were those for whom the scars of our childhood went deep. They all gave me the roots I needed to grow from in order to be able to nurture my own children. Silverlands was my family and my home for all my remembered childhood.

(Noël Coward wrote the following in December 1955, just before he relinquished his Presidency in 1956. It was discovered in the archives at TACT. I thought it a most fitting epilogue for my story. JS)

The Importance of Happiness

In this strange and difficult world there are, I fear, more unhappy people than happy ones. Not unhappy because of personal tragedy or loss of any specific circumstances, but unhappy in themselves, twisted, disgruntled, without confidence or hope or congenitally at odds with life. It is fairly simple as a rule to trace the first causes of this spiritual malaise directly back to early environment, in fact to childhood: for it is when we are very young children that we first learn to be afraid, and fear, of course, is the basis of much that is bad in human character.

I wonder, dear reader, how much you remember of your childhood? Possibly you seldom think of it, possibly it has become a vague memory submerged by the activities and responsibilities of adult life; but if, for a moment, you shut out the present and let your mind travel back across the years you will probably find many incidents and emotional crises, trivial enough in themselves, that have had a lasting effect on your present conduct, behaviour and attitude of mind.

Personally, I believe strongly that people who are brave, confident and successful are, nearly always, those whose early years were graced with happiness, with a sense of security and, above all, the knowledge of being loved and wanted.

The small children we take into the Actors' Orphanage have none of this security. Some of them may have loving mothers who are too poor to keep them, or affectionate fathers without the means of looking after them; some of them may have neither fathers nor mothers. None of them has a home in the accepted sense of the word and it is this that we try to give them. Somewhere safe and stable where birthdays and Christmases can be looked forward to with excitement and remembered with joy.

As President of the Actors' Orphanage I must, as part of the job, take an active interest in all sorts of things. Apart from the unending and vital task of raising money I am concerned with details of policy and of administration, with education, house repairs, estate development, the investment and reinvestment of capital and many different problems.

But in my heart what I really mind about, what I have minded about since I became President in 1934, is the happiness of the children who come into the care of this Charity.

It is my greatest hope that when these children have become men and women and look back into the past as I have asked my readers to do, they will be able to say: "Whatever has happened since, those were good years that I spent at Silverlands; throughout that time I was a happy child." That is my ideal, my dearest wish, and I am deeply grateful to anybody and everybody who helps to make it come true

Noël Coward, December 1955
President of The Actors' Orphanage Fund from 1934 – 1956

ABOUT THE TYPE IN THIS BOOK

Adobe Caslon was designed in 1990 by Carol Twombly,
and based on William Caslon's own specimen pages
printed between 1734 and 1770. The original Caslon is
cited as the first original typeface of English origin.

Geneva is a realist sans-serif typeface designed
in 1983 by Susan Kare for Apple Computer.